Star ★ Advertiser

A Taste of Aloha
FAVORITES

A Collection of Recipes from
The Junior League of Honolulu

Mutual Publishing

The Junior League of Honolulu, Inc. is an organization of women committed to promoting voluntarism, developing the potential of women, and improving communities through the effective action and leadership of trained volunteers.

The Junior League of Honolulu, Inc. reaches out to women of all races, religions, and national origins who demonstrate an interest in and commitment to voluntarism.

Copyright © 2019 by The Junior League of Honolulu, Inc.
All recipes are from previous cookbooks by The Junior League of Honolulu:
A Taste of Aloha © 1983, *Another Taste of Aloha* © 1993, and
Aloha Days Hula Nights © 2006.

Cover image © Pegge Hopper, painting titled *Walk Across the Sea.*

ISBN: 978-1-949307-09-2
Library of Congress Control Number: 2019943944

First Printing, September 2019

Mutual Publishing, LLC
1215 Center Street, Suite 210
Honolulu, Hawaii 96816
Ph: (808) 732-1709
Fax: (808) 734-4094
e-mail: info@mutualpublishing.com
www.mutualpublishing.com

Printed in South Korea

Contents

Star ★ Advertiser

The *Honolulu Star-Advertiser* knows well our readers enjoyment of both nostalgia and cooking. We remember the excitement created by the Junior League cookbooks when they first began appearing in the 1980s and continued to offer sumptuous recipes through the first decade of the twentieth century. Their publishing can be considered a seminal event in Island cookbook publishing, helping to bring Island cooking mainstream. This volume of favorite recipes, many still popular today, shows their timelessness and helps us to remember the rich diversity of Island cooking with its many ethnic flavors and influences.

The *Honolulu Star-Advertiser* is happy to bring back these dishes that preserve Hawai'i's past and foster Island cooking.

Dennis Francis

President and Publisher, *Honolulu Star-Advertiser*
and Oahu Publications Inc.

Foreword

I was both honored and flattered to be asked to select the recipes from the three best-selling *Taste of Aloha* cookbooks for *A Taste of Aloha Favorites.* The Junior League cookbooks were the rage of the day when they began appearing in the Islands and for almost twenty years dominated the island cookbook section in bookstores and kitchen shelves. Their recipe compilations reflected what was going on and being cooked in island homes—from traditional favorites to new twists on old recipes as well as then-considered nouveau cooking. Revisiting the cookbooks brought back a lot of cooking memories and reminded me of how good the recipes were and how varied and tasty Island cooking is.

Selecting recipes for this new anthology was difficult only because of the abundance of riches. The publisher had to keep telling me there was not room for every recipe to be included. I focused on dishes that are now regarded as classics and reflect the characteristics of Island food—our rich multiethnic heritage, fresh ingredients, ease of preparation, and of course, deliciousness. I put aside health trends although I stayed away from recipes that called for a lot of fat products. It amazes me how current the recipes still are even with all the culinary innovations that have occurred in Island cuisine. Good recipes don't lose much over time. They still retain their vitality and resonance.

— Muriel Miura, *editor*

Preface

The Junior League of Honolulu published its first cookbook, *A Taste of Aloha,* in 1983 to help raise money to support our community projects. The recipes showed our Islands' wide array of fresh seafood, crisp vegetables, and luscious fruits. Many were family favorites, handed down through generations. Others arrived in the islands with each new wave of settlers. All were suited to our relaxed island lifestyle and represent the varied influence of a wide world of cultures.

Two other volumes followed—*Another Taste of Aloha* and *Aloha Days Hula Nights.* All three books have been out of print for quite a while. We were surprised when the publisher approached us to do a compilation of the favorite recipes from all three volumes. It was flattering to hear that there was still interest in these books and peopled enjoyed the recipes even with the wave of culinary trends and emergence of local professional chefs that has since occurred.

Our recipes have been tested for quality and edited for clarity and consistency. The glossary at the back of the book will acquaint you with new cooking ingredients and methods of preparation. These words are noted throughout the book with asterisks (*). A fish chart will clarify our local names for various fish.

We hope you enjoy this anthology of the favorite recipes selected from all three volumes. We were excited that Muriel Miura, the grand dame of Island cooking, was to make the selection.

Enjoy and bon appetite.

The Junior League of Honolulu

The Junior League of Honolulu is an organization of women committed to promoting voluntarism, developing the potential of women, and improving communities through the effective action and leadership of trained volunteers. As women of diverse backgrounds, we are united in an effort to initiate significant change, build partnerships, and inspire shared solutions that will strengthen our island community.

Since 1923, the Junior League of Honolulu has been the impetus for creating positive social change in Honolulu. The Honolulu League's initial project was making layettes for Japanese earthquake victims. Later, League members were involved with improving the health of Honolulu's immigrant children through nutrition education at the community's Free Kindergartens. This award-winning program continued until it was turned over to the Community Chest in 1938.

Through the decades, the aloha spirit of assisting the community by identifying needs, providing volunteers, and developing services has encompassed the Arts, Historic Preservation, Advocacy, the Elderly, the Young, Consumer Rights, Foster Care, and Developing the Potential of Women.

Sales of our cookbooks, which began in the 1980s, help fund our important programs. Bringing back the favorite recipes will help to continue our important programs as part of the proceeds from sales will benefit Junior League activities.

Appetizers and Pūpū

Breadfruit Chips

Serves 4 to 6

The Island version of potato chips.

1 large ripe solid breadfruit,* about 3 pounds
Vegetable oil
Salt

Peel breadfruit. Wash under running cold water and dry. Cut into four sections and remove the core. Slice as thinly as possible. An electric slicer works best. In a deep fat fryer, heat oil to 350°F and cook breadfruit until it is light golden yellow. Drain on paper towels and salt immediately. Store chips in an airtight container. Chips may be frozen. Defrost at room temperature for 30 minutes, then heat in a warm oven. Serve with Chutney Guacamole.

Note: Breadfruit is ripe when white sap appears on the outside.

Hot Artichoke
and Spinach Dip

Serves 6 to 8

1 cup Parmesan cheese,* grated
1 cup mayonnaise
1 (10-ounce) package frozen spinach, thawed and drained
1 (6-ounce) jar marinated artichoke hearts, drained and
    chopped
1 (7-ounce) can green chilies, drained and chopped
½ teaspoon crushed red pepper
1 (2-ounce) jar pimento, chopped

Mix the cheese with the mayonnaise until well-blended. Add
the spinach, artichoke hearts, and green chilies to the mixture
and blend well. Spread mixture into 8-inch round cake pan
or divide into 2 oven-proof bowls. Sprinkle red pepper and
chopped pimento over top. Broil for 10 to 15 minutes or until
brown and dip is hot. Serve with crackers.

Crudité Dip

Makes 2 cups

1 cup mayonnaise
1 cup sour cream
1 tablespoon minced onion
1¼ tablespoons minced parsley
½ teaspoon garlic powder
1¼ tablespoons dill weed
1¼ teaspoons Beau Monde
½ teaspoon curry powder
Assorted vegetables

Blend first eight ingredients together. Arrange raw fresh vegetables in alternating colors: cauliflower rosettes, radishes, celery sticks, carrot sticks, cucumber sticks, sliced red and green bell peppers, blanched fresh asparagus, and mushroom caps.

Curried Paté

Makes 3 cups

1 pound liverwurst, softened
4 ounces cream cheese, softened
⅓ cup margarine, softened
1 tablespoon curry powder
3 tablespoons minced onion
3 tablespoons minced parsley
3 tablespoons brandy
Salt and pepper to taste

Combine liverwurst, cream cheese, and margarine in blender or food processor. Add remaining ingredients and blend well. Chill. Serve with melba toast, mild crackers, or Lavosh (see page 90).

Kim Chee Dip

Serves 4 to 6

8 ounces cream cheese, softened
½ cup chopped kim chee,* drained

In a food processor, combine cream cheese and kim chee and process until smooth. Chill. Serve with crackers or potato chips.

Chutney Guacamole

Makes 5 cups

The addition of chutney gives this extra zest!

4 ripe avocados, peeled and seeded
¼ cup chutney*
2 cloves garlic
2 to 3 small limes, juiced
Salt, pepper and cayenne to taste
1 cup chopped tomato

In a blender, place the meat of 3 avocados, the chutney, garlic, and lime juice. Season to taste. Add the chopped tomato and remaining avocado. Blend for 10 seconds. Chill and serve.

Albert Schmid
Executive Chef
Dillingham Corporation
Honolulu, Hawai'i

Island Curry Layers

Makes 4 cups

8 ounces cream cheese, softened
1 cup cottage cheese
¼ cup sour cream
2 teaspoons curry powder
1 cup Indian-style chutney*
⅓ cup green onions, chopped
⅓ cup raisins, chopped
⅓ cup coconut,* shredded
1 cup cooked chicken, chopped
½ cup salted peanuts, chopped

Combine cream cheese, cottage cheese, sour cream, and curry powder blending until smooth. Spread into serving dish. Top with chutney green onions, raisins, coconut, chicken, and peanuts. Cover and chill for 4 hours or overnight to blend flavors. Serve with assorted crackers.

Artichoke and Mushroom Spread

Makes 6 cups

2 baguettes, cut into ⅛-inch slices
1 tablespoon olive oil*
2 tablespoons butter
3 cloves garlic, minced
1 cup finely diced celery
2 pounds mushrooms, washed, stemmed, and diced
1 cup sliced green onions
3 cups diced marinated artichoke hearts
1½ teaspoons poultry seasoning
1 teaspoon minced fresh rosemary
Salt and black pepper
1 cup shredded Parmesan
1 cup shredded Romano

Heat oven to 350°F. Lay bread slices in single layer on a baking sheet. Toast lightly in oven. Put in a cloth lined basket. Set aside.

Heat oil and butter in a large frying pan over medium heat. Sauté garlic and celery until golden. Add mushrooms and sauté until tender, about 15 minutes. Drain off any liquid from mushrooms. Add green onions, artichoke hearts, poultry seasoning, and rosemary. Stir to mix and season with salt and pepper to taste. Heat thoroughly. Remove from heat, stir in Parmesan and Romano cheese. Place in chafing dish over low flame to keep warm, or scrape into baking dish, place in oven and bake 30 minutes. Serve warm with lightly toasted bread slices.

Savory Crab Cheesecake

Makes one 9-inch cake

2 pounds cream cheese softened
3 eggs
6 cloves garlic, passed through press
½ teaspoon salt
1 to 2 teaspoons hot pepper sauce,* such as Tabasco
1 tablespoon fresh lemon juice
1 pound fresh packed canned crabmeat
Sprigs of fresh parsley

Heat oven to 350°F. Grease a 9-inch springform pan and set aside. Beat cream cheese in a large mixing bowl until smooth. Beat in eggs one at a time, until well-blended. Stir in garlic, salt, pepper sauce, and lemon juice. Add crabmeat, mixing to blend. Pour into prepared pan and bake 45 to 55 minutes, until set. Place on wire rack to cool.

Remove from pan to serving plate, cover, and chill at least 2 hours. Remove from refrigerator 10 minutes before serving. Garnish with parsley. Serve with Ritz or Carr style crackers.

Note: Smoked or canned salmon can be used instead of crab.

Artichoke Balls

Makes 4 dozen

2 cloves garlic, minced
2 tablespoons olive oil*
2 (8-ounce) cans artichoke hearts, drained and chopped
2 eggs, slightly beaten
½ teaspoon cayenne
½ cup grated Parmesan cheese*
½ cup Italian-seasoned bread crumbs
¼ cup grated Parmesan cheese
¼ cup Italian-seasoned bread crumbs

Sauté garlic in oil but do not allow garlic to brown. Add artichokes, eggs, and cayenne and cook over low heat for 5 minutes. Remove from heat and add Parmesan cheese and bread crumbs. Using 1 teaspoon of mixture, make into balls and roll in second mixture of cheese and bread crumbs. Chill and serve.

Hawaiian "Artichoke" Cocktail

Serves 12

An Island surprise.

3 breadfruit,* baseball size
2 cups Caesar salad dressing
1 egg, hard cooked
Lettuce leaves

In a large pot, cover whole breadfruit with salted water and bring to a boil. Simmer for 1 hour and 45 minutes, keeping breadfruit submerged. Drain and cool. Peel, cut out centers and cut into bite-size pieces. Marinate overnight in Caesar dressing. Serve on a bed of lettuce and sprinkle with chopped egg.

Note: Breadfruit must be very immature.

Albert Schmid
Executive Chef
Dillingham Corporation
Honolulu, Hawai'i

Asian Fish Salad

Serves 12

1 pound fresh fish fillets, aʻu* or nairagi*
½ cup green onion, diced
1 cup Chinese parsley,* minced
½ cup pickled scallions,* sliced
¼ cup vegetable oil
4 teaspoons ginger,* freshly grated
¼ cup soy sauce*

Cut fish fillets across the grain in 2 x 1-inch slices and about ¼-inch thick. Arrange slices on serving platter in one layer. Top with green onion, Chinese parsley, and pickled scallions. Heat oil in saucepan until it begins to smoke, then remove pan from stove and let cool to room temperature.

Pour oil over fish. Serve with grated fresh ginger mixed with soy sauce as a dipping sauce.

Sushi Bar

Sushi may be compared to a Danish open-faced sandwich where one chooses from many toppings.

Basic Sushi Rice
3 cups short grained rice
3½ cups water
¾ to 1 cup rice vinegar*
½ to ⅔ cup sugar

In a heavy 3 to 4 quart pot, wash rice, stir, and drain. Repeat this procedure until water is clear. Add water to rice. Cover and bring to a boil. Reduce heat and simmer for 20 minutes. Turn off heat and let rice stand for 15 minutes. Transfer to large bowl. Combine vinegar and sugar and pour over rice. Mix with a wooden paddle. Cover rice with a damp cloth until ready to serve.

Sushi Toppings
20 (8 x 8) sheets sushi nori,* quartered
½ pound shrimp, cooked, shelled and deveined
½ pound crabmeat, cooked
½ pound sashimi,* thinly sliced
1 (6½-ounce) can tuna, drained and mixed with
    2 tablespoons soy sauce*
½ cup char siu* thinly sliced
1 pound kamaboko,* thinly sliced
1½ pounds steak, cooked and thinly sliced
1 avocado, peeled and thinly sliced
2 carrots, julienned and blanched
½ cup daikon* julienned
3½ ounces shiitake* mushrooms, soaked and thinly sliced
1 cup pickled ginger*
1 cucumber, julienned
½ cup chopped onion

¼ cup capers*
24 (3-inch) watercress* tips, blanched
8 ounces fresh mushrooms, sliced
2 egg omelet, thinly sliced
1 cup mayonnaise
¼ cup ume boshi*
¾ cup soy sauce*
4 tablespoons wasabi* powder combined with 2 teaspoons
    water to make a paste
1 lemon, thinly sliced and quartered

Arrange the toppings on a tray, alternating colors and textures to create an interesting presentation.

To assemble, place a nori square in the palm of the left hand. Spread rice on nori. Place a dab of wasabi on rice. Choose a layer of toppings, place on rice, and fold slightly with the right hand. Dip in soy sauce and eat.

Lumpia

This well-loved Filipino dish is a tasty combination of ingredients neatly wrapped in a thin dough and deep-fried.

½ pound ground pork
½ pound ground beef
½ cup chopped onion
½ pound raw shrimp, chopped
2 eggs, beaten
½ cup chopped mushrooms
½ cup grated carrot
¼ cup chopped green onion
2 cups shredded won bok*
3 cloves garlic, minced
2 tablespoons soy sauce*
Salt and pepper to taste
50 lumpia* wrappers*
Milk
Vegetable oil

In a large skillet, sauté pork, beef, and onion. Drain excess grease. Add shrimp to skillet and cook for 1 minute. Remove from heat. Add eggs, mushrooms, carrot, green onion, won bok, garlic, soy sauce, salt, and pepper. Set aside to cool. Put a heaping tablespoon of cooled mixture on each lumpia wrapper. Roll up, forming a small cylinder. Tuck ends into roll and seal wrapper with milk. Deep fry in oil until brown.

Note: Keep lumpia wrappers under a damp cloth. Lumpia wrappers will fall apart if mixture is not thoroughly cooled. Serve with Sweet Sour Lumpia Sauce (see page 15).

Sweet Sour Lumpia Sauce *Makes 2 cups*

1 cup water
½ cup sugar
¼ cup vinegar
½ cup catsup
2 teaspoons soy sauce*
Dash Tabasco
Salt and pepper to taste
2 tablespoons cornstarch
¼ cup water

In a saucepan, bring water, sugar, and vinegar to a boil. Add catsup, soy sauce, Tabasco, salt, and pepper. Dissolve cornstarch in water and add to sauce. Cook until thickened. Serve with Lumpia.

Thai Lettuce Rolls

Serves 3 to 4

7 to 8 leaves Mānoa,* or butter lettuce
5 to 6 slices cucumber, seeded
4 (½-inch) cubes firm tofu,* drained
4 (¼-inch) strips red bell pepper
4 (¼-inch) strips green bell pepper
4 (¼-inch) strips yellow bell pepper
2 tablespoons bean sprouts*
5 to 6 leaves mint
5 to 6 leaves basil
2 sprigs Chinese parsley*
Kampyo* *(see note)*
Peanuts, finely chopped

Dressing
⅓ cup lime juice
6 ounces fish sauce*
1 stalk (bottom part only) lemon grass,* sliced thin, crosswise
2 serrano chilies, finely diced
3 cups water
¾ cup sugar
1 teaspoon dried red chili, crushed

Combine dressing ingredients and stir until sugar is dissolved. Let stand one day before serving. Top dressing with peanuts immediately before serving. Lay 3 or 4 leaves of lettuce with edges slightly overlapping on a plate. Layer half of cucumber tofu, peppers, bean sprouts, mint, and basil on lettuce. Roll lettuce to create a bun, leaving ends open. Tie with kampyo. Repeat. Place two lettuce rolls on a plate. Garnish with Chinese parsley. Serve with dressing on the side for dipping.

Note: Dried kampyo may be simmered in equal parts of water and chicken stock until tender.

Papaya Spring Rolls

Makes 2 dozen

½ cup chunky peanut butter
⅓ cup water
2 tablespoons rice vinegar*
2 tablespoons fish sauce* *(see note)*
2 teaspoons hot chili paste
2 large firm ripe papayas*
1 long unpeeled Japanese cucumber*
24 (6-inch diameter) rice paper rounds
24 large fresh basil leaves
48 large fresh mint leaves
48 small fresh cilantro* sprigs

In a medium bowl, whisk together peanut butter, water, vinegar, fish sauce, and chili paste. Cover and chill. Whisk again before serving. This can be made the day before. Halve papaya lengthwise, peel, and remove seeds. Cut each piece in half crosswise then into ½-inch thick strips and set aside. Cut cucumber into ¼-inch thick strips 2½ inches long. Set aside.

Fill a shallow baking pan with warm water. Working in batches, soak 2 to 3 rice paper rounds in water until softened, about 2 minutes. Remove rounds from water and arrange in single layer on clean dish towel. Place 1 basil leaf in center of each round vein side up. Place 2 mint leaves on top of each basil leaf, again vein side up. Place 2 papaya strips, then 2 cucumber strips parallel on top of mint. Arrange 2 cilantro sprigs on top of cucumber. Fold one parallel edge (to papaya-cucumber) of each round over filling. Fold in sides and roll up rice paper rounds tightly, enclosing filling. Transfer to platter. Repeat with remaining rounds. Cover with moist paper towel, wrap in plastic, and chill. These can be made up to eight hours ahead. Keep tightly wrapped and chilled. Serve rolls with peanut sauce.

Note: Fish sauce has a very pungent, salty taste, and is an essential ingredient in many Asian dishes. In Vietnam, it is called nuoc nam; in Thailand, nam pla; and in the Philippines, patis. Fish sauce and rice flour* wrappers known as banh trang are available at Asian markets and in the Asian foods section of some supermarkets.

Sweet and Sour Chicken Wings

Serves 12

5 pounds chicken wings or drumettes
4 eggs, beaten
2 cups cornstarch
½ cup vegetable oil
2 teaspoons garlic salt
1 teaspoon freshly ground black pepper
1 teaspoon salt

Preheat oven to 350°F. Cut each chicken wing into 3 sections. Reserve the wing tips to make stock. Dip the other chicken pieces in beaten eggs. Roll each piece in cornstarch and fry until golden brown. Transfer chicken to baking dishes. Mix garlic salt, pepper, and salt together and sprinkle evenly over chicken.

Sauce
½ cup chicken stock
1 cup sugar
1 cup cider vinegar
6 tablespoons catsup
2 tablespoons soy sauce*
2 teaspoons salt

Combine the ingredients and pour over chicken. Bake for 30 minutes.

Note: This can be made up to 3 days ahead. Reheat before serving.

Tūtū's Chicken Delight

Serves 6

Tūtū is the Hawaiian nickname for grandmother.

3½ pounds drummettes
Salt
½ to ¾ cup cornstarch
Vegetable oil
2 cups water
2 cups soy sauce*
¾ cup brown sugar
3 tablespoons sesame oil*
3 tablespoons sesame seeds*
3 green onions, finely chopped
Garnish: sesame seeds* and chopped green onions

Lightly salt drummettes and roll in cornstarch. Stir fry in oil until light brown. Drain. Combine water, soy sauce, brown sugar, sesame oil, sesame seeds, and green onions in a shallow pan. Marinate drummettes in mixture for 1 hour at room temperature. Drain and broil until brown and crispy about 10 minutes per side. Sprinkle with sesame seeds and chopped green onions. Serve hot or cold.

Teriyaki Sausage

Serves 10

2 pounds mild or hot Portuguese sausage*
¾ cup soy sauce*
1¼ cups sugar
1 tablespoon chopped fresh ginger*

Cut Portuguese sausage into ¼-inch slices. Combine remaining ingredients in a saucepan. Add sausage and simmer for 35 minutes. Serve hot with toothpicks.

Stilton Cocktail Puffs *Makes about 3 dozen*

4 slices bacon
½ cup water
4 tablespoons unsalted butter
½ cup all-purpose flour
2 eggs
1 cup crumbled Stilton
2 green onions, minced
¼ teaspoon black pepper

Heat a small skillet over medium heat. Add bacon and cook until crisp. Remove from pan, drain on paper towel. Let cool and crumble. Heat oven to 425 °F. Lightly grease two baking sheets and set aside. Cut butter into pieces. In a small heavy saucepan, combine water and butter. Bring to a boil over high heat. Reduce heat to medium, add the flour all at once, and beat with a wooden spoon until mixture pulls away from the sides of pan and forms a ball. Remove pan from heat.

Add eggs one at a time, beating well after each addition. Stir in Stilton until blended. Add bacon and green onion, season with pepper. Drop rounded teaspoonfuls of batter 2 inches apart on prepared baking sheets. Bake in middle of oven for 15 to 20 minutes until crisp and golden. Serve immediately.

Note: The dough can be made several hours ahead, but do not bake until ready to serve.

Salads and Salad Dressings

Salads

Salad Dressings

The Bistro's Caesar Salad
Serves 2

A favorite from the Bistro at Diamond Head.

½ teaspoon salt
1 clove garlic
Juice of ½ lemon
2 tablespoons wine vinegar*
1 teaspoon Dijon mustard*
⅓ teaspoon anchovy paste
1 coddled egg
¼ teaspoon freshly ground black pepper
3 teaspoons Worcestershire sauce
3 to 4 tablespoons olive oil*
1 head romaine lettuce, torn in bite-size pieces
¼ cup shredded Parmesan cheese*
Croutons

"First take the wooden bowl, sprinkle salt in the bottom. Impale garlic clove on fork and rub (gently) around (the garlic clove, that is!). Take half a lemon and squeeze into bowl. Now, remove lemon pips and any garlic that may be left in bowl. Sprinkle wine vinegar to augment juice of lemon; more vinegar for a dry lemon, less for a juicy one. Place a teaspoon of mustard (make it a good one), a third teaspoon of anchovy paste (be careful, this stuff is very salty). At this point, take the egg that should be in the hot water (and if it's not, you're going to be) and break it into the bowl. Grind 15 to 20 turns of pepper over yolk of egg. (This will enable you to see how much pepper is coming out of the grinder.) Turn a bottle of Worcestershire sauce upside down and encircle bowl three times (approximately 3 teaspoons). While mixing this entire mess, smile and add three or four tablespoons (wooden mixing spoon) full of olive oil. Mix well. Add romaine lettuce and 2 generous spoons of Parmesan cheese. Toss. Put on salad plates. Sprinkle with croutons. Serve!"

Basic Spinach Salad

Serves 4 to 6

2 bunches spinach, washed, trimmed, and torn in bite-size
    pieces
½ pound bacon, fried and crumbled
2 hard-cooked eggs, chopped
1 cup sliced fresh mushrooms

Dressing
1 egg
1 tablespoon finely grated Parmesan cheese*
2 tablespoons Dijon mustard*
3 tablespoons lemon juice
1 teaspoon Worcestershire sauce
1 tablespoon sugar
½ teaspoon salt
Dash white pepper
¼ cup vegetable oil

Prepare salad ingredients. Blend the dressing ingredients except
the oil. Add oil and beat thoroughly. Store in the refrigerator
if not used immediately. Combine spinach, bacon, egg, and
mushrooms. Add dressing and toss lightly.

Spinach Salad with Chutney Dressing

Serves 2 to 4

1 pound fresh spinach, trimmed and torn in bite-size pieces
6 fresh mushrooms, sliced
1 cup water chestnuts* sliced
6 slices bacon, fried and crumbled
⅓ to ½ cup shredded Gruyère cheese

Dressing

¼ cup wine vinegar*
1 clove garlic, minced
2 to 3 tablespoons chutney*
2 teaspoons sugar
2 tablespoons coarsely ground Dijon mustard*
⅓ to ½ cup vegetable oil
Salt and freshly ground black pepper to taste

In a blender, combine dressing ingredients except the oil. Blend until smooth. Add the oil, blend, and adjust seasonings. Refrigerate. Bring dressing to room temperature before serving. Combine salad ingredients. Pour dressing over salad, toss and serve.

Spinach Salad with
Warm Cranberry Dressing *Serves 4*

Dressing
1 cup cranberry relish
2 tablespoons granulated sugar
1 teaspoon salt
1 teaspoon black pepper
1 tablespoon grated fresh ginger* root
Dash or two ground nutmeg
2 cups walnut or olive oil*

Salad
2 pounds fresh spinach leaves, washed and stemmed
½ to ¾ cup walnut halves
15 ounces canned Mandarin orange* sections, drained well
½ cup crumbled feta cheese*

Cranberry Relish
12-ounce bag fresh cranberries
1 orange, quartered with peel
3 tablespoons sugar

Place cranberry relish in blender or food processor. Add sugar, salt, pepper, ginger, and nutmeg. Pulse to combine. With machine running, slowly add oil until well-blended. Scrape into saucepan. Heat over low heat until warmed through.

In a salad bowl, toss spinach with half the warm dressing. Add walnuts, orange sections, and feta. Serve with additional dressing and remaining relish on the side.

Cranberry Relish: Place cranberries, orange, and sugar in blender or food processor. Pulse until finely chopped, about 30 seconds. Scrape into container, cover, and chill until ready to use.

Green Mango Salad   *Serves 4*

2 large green mangoes,* just starting to ripen
1 tablespoon vegetable oil
½ teaspoon mustard seeds
1 small fresh red chili, finely minced with seeds
15 ounces canned black beans,* drained
3 tablespoons shredded coconut*
2 teaspoons soy sauce*
1 small head of Mānoa or red leaf lettuce, washed and patted
    dry
1 large ripe avocado, peeled and diced

Peel mangoes. Grate into a mixing bowl and set aside. Discard seed. Heat oil in saucepan over medium heat. Add mustard seeds and chili. When mustard seeds start to pop, add mango, beans, coconut, and soy sauce. Sauté, stirring frequently, about 5 minutes until heated through.

Slice lettuce into thin strips and spread in shallow bowl. Mound mango mixture in center. Sprinkle with avocado. Serve.

Note: The texture of this dish is softer than a green papaya salad and the green mango has a tangier flavor.

Green Papaya Salad

Serves 2 to 4

1 clove garlic
1 to 3 Hawaiian chili peppers*
½ pound green papaya* peeled, seeded and shredded
1 tomato, sliced
2 tablespoons Thai fish sauce*
3 tablespoons lime juice
1 head lettuce or cabbage, shredded

Grind garlic with chili peppers. Combine shredded papaya, sliced tomato, fish sauce, lime juice, and pepper-garlic mixture and mix well. Serve with lettuce or cabbage.

Keo Sananikone
Keo's
Honolulu, Hawai'i

Papaya Salad

1 small Maui onion,* thinly sliced
1 semi-ripe papaya* peeled, seeded, and cubed
1 bunch watercress,* trimmed and cut in 1-inch pieces
Lettuce leaves

Dressing
⅓ cup tarragon vinegar*
1 tablespoon honey
1 tablespoon poppy seeds
1 tablespoon chopped fresh mint
½ teaspoon ground coriander
Dash white pepper

Soak onion in a bowl of water for 10 minutes. Drain. Add papaya and refrigerate for 1 hour. Combine dressing ingredients. Toss papaya, onion, and watercress with dressing. Serve on bed of lettuce.

Hearts of Palm Salad
Serves 6

1 (16-ounce) can hearts of palm, drained and cut in ½-inch
    pieces
6 cups romaine lettuce, torn into bite-size pieces

Dressing
1 cup olive oil*
½ cup vinegar
½ cup celery, finely chopped
¼ cup red bell pepper, finely chopped
¼ cup onion, finely chopped
¼ cup dill pickles, finely chopped
6 black olives, finely chopped
2 cloves garlic, pressed
¼ teaspoon capers*

Combine dressing ingredients. Chill at least 8 hours. Arrange
lettuce on individual serving plates and top with hearts of palm
pieces. Pour dressing over salad and serve.

Macadamia Nut Pea Salad   *Serves 6*

1 (16-ounce) package frozen peas
1 cup celery, chopped
¼ cup green onions, including 3 to 4 inches of green tops, chopped
1 cup macadamia nuts* or cashews, chopped
¼ cup bacon, fried crisp and crumbled
1 cup sour cream
½ teaspoon salt
¼ cup Dressing
Boston or Mānoa* lettuce leaves

Dressing
1½ teaspoons lemon juice
½ cup red wine vinegar*
1 teaspoon salt
½ teaspoon freshly ground pepper
1½ teaspoons Worcestershire sauce
½ teaspoon Dijon mustard*
1 clove garlic, crushed
2 tablespoons sugar
1½ teaspoons grated onion and juice
1½ cups corn oil

Blend the dressing ingredients except the oil. Add oil and beat thoroughly. Store in the refrigerator if not used immediately. Turn frozen peas into a colander and rinse until thawed. Drain. Combine peas, celery, onion, nuts, and bacon. Mix sour cream, salt, and ¼ cup dressing and pour over salad, mixing lightly. Cover and chill, preferably overnight. Serve on a bed of lettuce. Remaining dressing may be refrigerated for later use.

Onion juice is obtained by grating a large white onion on the fine side of a grater or processing it in an electric blender and straining the purée.

Kim Chee Salad

Serves 10 to 15

1 head cabbage, cut in bite-size pieces
¼ cup coarse salt
1 small carrot, julienned
4 green onions, sliced
5 cloves garlic, minced
½ cup cider vinegar
1½ teaspoons cayenne or crushed red pepper
2 teaspoons sesame oil*
2 teaspoons toasted sesame seeds*
4 tablespoons vegetable oil
3 teaspoons sugar

Sprinkle salt over cabbage, toss and set aside for 20 minutes. Rinse and drain cabbage in salad dryer. In large bowl, combine cabbage with vegetables and seasonings. Toss well. Refrigerate and toss at intervals to blend flavors.

Note: The longer this sits, the better the flavor.

Chinese Chicken Salad *Serves 10*

10 boneless chicken breasts, skinned
2 cups julienned ham
1 cucumber, peeled, seeded and julienned
⅓ cup chopped peanuts
2 green onions, thinly sliced
1 small head iceberg lettuce, shredded

Dressing
4 tablespoons peanut butter
3 tablespoons soy sauce*
1 tablespoon dry mustard
3 tablespoons cider vinegar
½ teaspoon salt
1 teaspoon toasted sesame seeds*
3 cloves garlic, minced
¼ teaspoon white pepper
¼ teaspoon crushed red pepper

Simmer chicken breasts in water until tender. Cool. Shred by hand to make approximately 5 cups. Mix dressing ingredients in a bowl. Pour over chicken and ham. Mix until well-coated. Add cucumber, peanuts, and green onion. Toss. Place lettuce on individual plates and divide chicken salad equally.

Mandarin Almond Salad   *Serves 4 to 6*

Excellent as a complement to a curry.

3 tablespoons sugar
½ cup silvered almonds
1 head romaine lettuce, torn in bite-size pieces
½ head iceberg lettuce, torn in bite-size pieces
1 cup chopped green onions
¾ cup chopped celery
1 (11-ounce) can mandarin oranges,* drained

Dressing
2 tablespoons cider vinegar
¼ cup vegetable oil
2 tablespoons chopped fresh parsley
½ teaspoon salt
Dash Tabasco
1 tablespoon brown sugar (optional)

In a saucepan over medium heat, melt the sugar until pale caramel in color. Add almonds and stir to coat. Remove from heat and pour on foil to cool. Chop when cooled. Set aside. In a large salad bowl, combine the lettuce leaves, onions, and celery. Refrigerate two hours or overnight to enhance flavor. In a small bowl, mix the dressing ingredients and refrigerate. When ready to serve, add the almonds, oranges, and dressing to the lettuce and toss.

Hearty Lentil Salad

Serves 10

1 pound lentils
3 carrots, diced
½ pound smoked turkey, diced
6 large green onions, chopped
4 cups mixed salad greens

Dressing
2 large cloves garlic
1 cup fresh parsley
⅓ cup vegetable oil
¼ cup fresh lemon juice
¼ cup red wine vinegar*
2 tablespoons Dijon mustard*
1 teaspoon salt
1 teaspoon grated lemon zest
½ teaspoon freshly ground pepper

Bring a large saucepan of lightly salted water to a boil. Add lentils and simmer until crisp-tender, about 20 to 30 minutes. Add carrots and simmer for 2 more minutes. Meanwhile, mince garlic in a food processor. Add parsley and finely chop. Add remaining dressing ingredients and process until blended. Drain lentils and combine with turkey and green onions. Pour dressing over lentils and turkey and toss to coat. Arrange greens on individual plates and divide lentil salad equally. Serve warm.

Somen Noodle Salad

Serves 10

This colorful salad is an excellent buffet or picnic dish.

2 (9-ounce) packages somen noodles,* boiled and rinsed with
    cold water
½ head iceberg lettuce, shredded
½ pound char siu * or ham, sliced into strips
2 egg omelet, julienned
1 cucumber, sliced into strips
1 package kamaboko* sliced into strips
1 (7-ounce) can crabmeat, shredded (optional)
4 green onions, finely chopped
2 cups fresh watercress,* cut in 2-inch pieces

Dressing

⅓ cup rice vinegar*
1 tablespoon vegetable oil
1 tablespoon sesame oil*
½ cup soy sauce*
¼ cup sugar
2 tablespoons sesame seeds*
Garnish: Chinese parsley* and sliced water chestnuts*

Toss the salad with dressing and serve.

Hearts of Palm and Crab   *Serves 6*

Dressing
1 medium firm ripe avocado, peeled, seeded, and cubed
⅔ cup buttermilk
¼ cup sour cream
3 tablespoons minced sweet onion
2½ tablespoons fresh lime juice
2 tablespoons olive oil*
1 teaspoon minced garlic
1 teaspoon minced fresh dill or ½ teaspoon dried
½ teaspoon salt
⅛ teaspoon cayenne pepper

Salad
1 head Butter or Mānoa lettuce*, separated, washed and pat-
    ted dry
2 large vine-ripened tomatoes, thinly sliced
¾ pound fresh hearts of palm, trimmed and poached until
    tender or 14 ounces jarred or canned; drained and cut into
    ¼-inch slices
1 pound fresh or canned crab, picked through to remove carti-
    lage or shell

Place avocado in a mixing bowl and mash well. Beat in
buttermilk and sour cream. Stir in onion, lime juice, oil, garlic,
dill, salt, and cayenne. Cover and refrigerate until ready to use.
This can be done up to 4 hours in advance. Dressing can be
made in a blender for a smoother texture.

Lay lettuce leaves overlapping on each of six large plates. Fan
out equal amounts of tomato slices on the lettuce. Scatter with
hearts of palm slices. Mound crabmeat in the center. Drizzle
dressing over all and serve.

Curried Tuna Salad

Makes 3 cups

1 (6⅛-ounce) can chunk light tuna, drained and flaked
½ cup celery, diced
½ cup carrot, diced
½ cup raisins
½ cup walnuts, chopped
¼ cup green onion, chopped
½ cup Swiss cheese, grated
1 teaspoon fresh parsley, chopped
2 tablespoons sweet pickle relish
½ cup plus 2 tablespoons mayonnaise
2 teaspoons Dijon mustard*
¼ teaspoon freshly ground pepper
½ teaspoon salt
½ teaspoon curry powder
½ cup black olives, coarsely chopped
1 green bell pepper, chopped (optional)
1 red bell pepper, chopped (optional)
6 hard-cooked eggs, chopped (optional)
Garnish: parsley and alfalfa sprouts

Mix all ingredients. Cover and chill for 1 to 2 hours. Salad may be served with crackers or vegetables, stuffed into cucumbers or cherry tomatoes, or used as a sandwich spread.

Stuff tuna mixture into hollowed-out cucumber slices or cherry tomatoes using a melon baller or a small spoon.

Cold Steak Salad

Serves 8

This salad serves four as an entrée.

2 pounds boneless sirloin steak, cut about 2 inches thick
Salt and freshly ground pepper
½ pound mushrooms, sliced
½ cup scallions, sliced
1 (14-ounce) can hearts of palm, drained and sliced
2 tablespoons chives, chopped
2 tablespoons parsley, chopped
2 teaspoons dried dill
1 head romaine lettuce

Dressing
1 egg (see Note)
½ cup olive oil*
3 tablespoons tarragon* or white wine vinegar*
4 teaspoons Dijon mustard*
1 teaspoon salt
2 teaspoons lemon juice
1 teaspoon Worcestershire sauce
Dash Tabasco
Garnish: 2 medium tomatoes, sliced

Season both sides of the steak with salt and pepper. Broil until medium-rare, about 8 to 10 minutes per side. Cool slightly and cut into ⅛-inch slices. Combine remaining salad ingredients and mix with steak slices. To prepare dressing, place the egg in a food processor or blender. With motor running, slowly add oil. Add remaining ingredients and blend well. Pour over steak salad and mix until well-coated. Garnish. Serve cold or at room temperature.

Note: Egg substitute may be used instead of the raw egg in the dressing. Freeze the steak slightly for ease in cutting.

Celery Seed Dressing

½ cup cider vinegar
1 tablespoon Dijon mustard*
1 teaspoon celery seed
½ teaspoon Worcestershire sauce
1 egg
3 teaspoons sugar
1½ teaspoons salt
¼ teaspoon white pepper
1 clove garlic, minced
1 teaspoon sweet relish
½ teaspoon Kitchen Bouquet
½ teaspoon Maggi seasoning
Juice of ½ lemon
2 cups vegetable oil

Combine vinegar, mustard, celery seed, Worcestershire, egg, sugar, salt, pepper, garlic, relish, Kitchen Bouquet, Maggi seasoning, and lemon. Blend oil in slowly.

Maile Room
Kahala Hilton
Honolulu, Hawai'i

Creamy Louis Dressing *Makes 2½ cups*

Excellent on crab, shrimp, chicken or tuna salad.

1 cup mayonnaise
⅓ cup chili sauce
3 tablespoons pickle relish
3 tablespoons finely chopped green pepper
2 tablespoons finely chopped celery
¼ teaspoon paprika
¼ to ½ teaspoon salt
Dash Tabasco
½ cup whipping cream, whipped

Combine all ingredients except cream. Blend well. Fold in whipped cream. Cover and chill until ready to serve. Store for up to 4 days.

Ginger Salad Dressing *Makes 1½ cups*

2-inch piece fresh ginger,* peeled
3 cloves garlic
½ cup parsley
2 tablespoons Dijon mustard*
2 tablespoons honey
1½ teaspoons salt
½ teaspoon pepper
¼ cup cider or wine vinegar*
¾ cup vegetable oil

In a food processor, mince the fresh ginger and garlic. Add remaining ingredients and blend well.

Green Goddess Salad Dressing

Makes 1½ cups

2 teaspoons tarragon vinegar*
3 tablespoons chopped parsley
3 tablespoons chopped green onion
2 teaspoons anchovy fillets
2 teaspoons chives
1 teaspoon capers*
1 clove garlic
⅛ teaspoon salt
1 cup mayonnaise

Combine ingredients except mayonnaise in a food processor. Process. Add mayonnaise and process thoroughly. Chill for two hours.

Papaya Seed Dressing

Makes 1 cup

Excellent on your favorite fruit or green salad.

¼ cup tarragon vinegar*
¼ cup sugar
¼ teaspoon salt
½ teaspoon dry mustard
½ cup vegetable oil
½ small onion, finely chopped
1 tablespoon fresh papaya* seeds

Put vinegar and dry ingredients in a blender. With motor running, add oil in a steady stream and add onion. Add papaya seeds and blend only until the seeds resemble coarsely ground pepper. Chill for 1 hour before serving

Waioli Guava Dressing   *Makes 3 cups*

1 cup mayonnaise
1 cup catsup
¼ cup vinegar
½ cup vegetable oil
1 teaspoon dry mustard
2 teaspoons lemon juice
½ cup guava* jelly or jam
½ teaspoon garlic salt

Combine ingredients and beat until well-blended. Chill.

Waioli Tea Room
Honolulu, Hawai'i

Maui Onion Salad Dressing   *Makes ¾ cup*

1 clove garlic, pressed
¼ Maui onion,* sliced
½ cup vegetable oil
¼ cup sugar
¼ cup vinegar
1 bay leaf, crumbled
1 teaspoon salt
¼ teaspoon prepared mustard
⅛ teaspoon freshly ground pepper
⅛ teaspoon Worcestershire sauce

In a food processor mince garlic and Maui onion. Add remaining ingredients and blend until smooth. Chill for one hour before serving.

Papaya Seed Dressing 2   *Makes ¾ cup*

Excellent on spinach salad.

½ cup mayonnaise
2 tablespoons vinegar
2 tablespoons sugar
1 small clove garlic
1 tablespoon fresh papaya seeds*

Mix vinegar mayonnaise and sugar in a blender. With motor running, add onion. Add papaya seeds and blend until the seeds resemble coarsely ground pepper. Chill for 1 hour before serving.

Poppy Seed French Dressing

Makes 2 cups

1 cup sugar
1 cup vegetable oil
½ cup white vinegar
1 teaspoon dry mustard
1 teaspoon celery seed
1 teaspoon paprika
1 teaspoon poppy seeds
1 teaspoon salt
3 tablespoons onion, grated

Combine all ingredients in blender. Blend until sugar is dissolved. Chill.

Tofu Dressing

Makes 4 cups

12 ounces soft tofu,* drained
4 tablespoons vegetable oil
3 tablespoons lemon juice
2 cloves garlic, minced
½ to 1 teaspoon salt
Dash white pepper
1 tablespoon freshly grated Parmesan* or Romano cheese*

In a food processor or blender, process tofu, slowly adding oil and lemon juice. Add garlic, seasonings and cheese. Blend and chill.

Bacon Dressing

4 slices bacon, fried and crumbled, reserve drippings
3 tablespoons white wine vinegar*
2 tablespoons sugar
1 egg, beaten
Salt and pepper to taste

Cool bacon drippings slightly and add vinegar, sugar, and egg. Whisk vigorously until thickened. Add bacon and stir. Season and serve over lettuce, spinach, or vegetable salad.

Soups

Miso Soup from the P.K. *Serves 10*

7 cups water
1 handful hana katsuo*
5 ounces aka miso*
4 ounces shiro miso*
Garnish: chopped green onion and cubed tofu*

Bring water to a boil and turn off heat. Add hana katsuo and let stand 2 minutes, then strain. Add aka miso and shiro miso. Stir well. Heat thoroughly but do not boil. Garnish and serve.

Princess Kaiulani Hotel
Honolulu, Hawai'i

Pearl Barley Soup *Serves 8*

¾ cup pearl barley
3 cups chicken broth
3 tablespoons butter
1½ cups onion, minced
1 cup carrot, minced
1 cup mushrooms, thinly sliced
½ cup celery, minced
8 cups chicken stock
Salt and freshly ground pepper to taste
Garnish: sour cream, sliced mushrooms, and chopped parsley

Bring barley and 3 cups chicken broth to a boil in a small saucepan. Reduce heat and simmer for 1 hour or until the liquid is absorbed. Sauté onion, carrot, mushrooms, and celery in butter until tender. Add remaining chicken stock and simmer for 25 minutes. Add barley and simmer for five more minutes. Garnish and serve.

Fresh Mushroom Bisque   *Serves 6*

½ pound butter
¾ pound fresh mushrooms, sliced
1 clove garlic, minced
½ cup chopped onion
2 tablespoons lemon juice
4 tablespoons flour
4 cups chicken broth
1½ teaspoons salt
¼ teaspoon pepper
2 cups half-and-half
Garnish: fresh parsley

Sauté mushrooms, garlic, and onion in butter for 3 minutes. Add lemon juice. Mix flour in a small amount of the chicken broth to prevent lumps and add along with the remaining ingredients to the mushroom mixture. Simmer for 15 minutes. Do not boil. Garnish and serve.

Artichoke Bowls   *Serves 6*

A unique soup that must be made ahead.

6 fresh artichokes
12 ounces French or Italian salad dressing
1½ cups chilled consommé
6 tablespoons sour cream
3 tablespoons caviar
Sour cream for dipping

Cook artichokes until tender. Spread artichoke open and remove choke. Pour 1 to 2 tablespoons of salad dressing into the center of each artichoke. Let stand several hours or refrigerate overnight. Fill each artichoke with ¼ cup chilled consommé. Top with 1 tablespoon of sour cream and ½ teaspoon of caviar. Serve on individual plates with additional sour cream for the leaves.

Pumpkin Coconut Bisque *Serves 4 to 6*

2 tablespoons butter
1 cup chopped onion
6 cloves garlic, minced
½ small fresh hot red chili, minced or ½ teaspoon dried
    crushed red pepper flakes
½ teaspoon ground allspice
Dash ground cinnamon
2 teaspoons granulated sugar
2 cups chicken broth
3 cups canned solid pack pumpkin
1½ cups canned coconut milk*
Salt and black pepper
Shredded coconut*
Ground nutmeg

Melt butter in a large, heavy saucepan over medium heat. Add onion, garlic, and chili. Sauté until onion is golden, about 8 minutes. Add allspice, cinnamon, and sugar. Cook 30 seconds, stirring to blend flavors. Scrape into a blender or food processor. Add a little of the chicken broth and purée until smooth. Add pumpkin and blend well. Return to pot. Stir in remaining chicken broth. Bring to a boil over medium-high heat. Reduce heat to medium-low, cover and simmer to blend flavors, about 30 minutes.

Just before serving, thin soup with coconut milk to desired consistency. Season to taste with salt and pepper. Heat through without bringing to a boil. Ladle soup into bowls and sprinkle with coconut and nutmeg. Serve.

Note: This soup can be made a day ahead and kept covered in refrigerator without losing any of its richness. Coconut milk can be found in Asian specialty stores and in supermarkets that carry Asian products.

Hot and Sour Soup

6 cups chicken stock
⅓ pound lean pork butt, slivered
6 dried mushrooms, soaked to soften and julienned
½ cup bamboo shoots,* julienned
½ cup water chestnuts,* sliced
1 teaspoon minced fresh ginger*
½ cup cloud ears,* soaked to soften
1 pound firm tofu,* cut into small cubes
1 tablespoon soy sauce*
1 tablespoon rice wine*
2 tablespoons rice vinegar*
½ teaspoon white pepper
Salt to taste
1 egg, beaten
2 tablespoons chopped green onion
½ teaspoon sesame oil*
½ teaspoon chili oil* (optional)

Bring stock to a boil, add pork, mushrooms, bamboo shoots, water chestnuts, ginger, and cloud ears. Reduce heat and simmer for 10 minutes. Add tofu, soy sauce, rice wine, rice vinegar, and pepper. Bring back to a boil. Season and remove from heat. Slowly pour in egg, stirring constantly. Add green onion, sesame oil, and chili oil. Serve immediately.

Chinese Oxtail Soup

Serves 10

5 pounds oxtails, cut in sections
½ cup raw shelled peanuts, blanched
3 (14-ounce) cans beef broth (chicken broth
    may be substituted)
1 small piece kwo pee*
1 clove garlic, minced
½ to 1 inch piece fresh ginger* peeled and crushed
1 small piece star anise* (approximately 3 spokes)
2 green onions
1 stalk celery
¼ cup whiskey
½ teaspoon salt
½ teaspoon garlic salt
1 cup fresh watercress,* cut in 2-inch pieces
Garnish: minced green onions, minced Chinese parsley,*
    grated fresh ginger*

In a large pot, parboil oxtails in water for 5 minutes. Drain. Add
remaining ingredients except for watercress and garnish. Cover
and simmer for 3 hours or until oxtails are tender. Remove
and discard green onions and celery. Chill soup overnight
(or in freezer for a few hours) and remove congealed fat. Add
watercress and reheat before serving. Garnish.

Vietnamese Pho

5 pounds beef marrow or knuckle bones
2 pounds beef chuck, cut into two pieces
6 quarts water, divided
3-inch piece fresh ginger* root, cut lengthwise and lightly
    bruised
2 yellow onions peeled and quartered
¼ cup fish sauce*
3 tablespoons granulated sugar
6 whole star anise*
3 whole cloves
1 tablespoon sea salt
10 ounces rice noodles
⅓ pound beef sirloin, slightly frozen
Scallions, cilantro,* bean sprouts,* herbs, chilies, lime juice,
    and black pepper

Cleanse bones and beef chuck by placing in a pot of water, bringing to a boil over high heat and boiling vigorously for 5 minutes. Transfer bones and beef chuck to a fresh soup pot filled with 4 quarts water. Bring to a boil. Reduce heat to medium-low and simmer, skimming the surface often to remove any foam and fat.

Place ginger and onions over hot grill or under broiler and char lightly. Add the charred ginger and onions, fish sauce, and sugar to soup pot. Simmer about 60 minutes. Up to two more quarts of water can be added if needed.

Lightly toast star anise in a dry pan. Wrap star anise and cloves in a spice bag or piece of cheesecloth. When the broth has been simmering for about 1½ hours, add spice bag. Let infuse until the broth is fragrant, about 30 to 40 minutes.

Remove and discard both the spice bag and onions. Stir in salt.

The broth will taste salty but will be balanced once the noodles and accompaniments are added. Remove one piece of chuck, drain, cut into thin slices, and set aside. Let the other piece of chuck and bones continue to simmer in the pot while the noodles are prepared and the bowls are assembled.

Cover rice noodles with cold water. Soak 20 minutes, then drain. Bring 3 cups water to a boil in a medium saucepan over high heat. Add noodles and cook 3 to 5 minutes until tender. Drain, keep warm.

Slice slightly frozen beef paper-thin across the grain. Place the cooked noodles in large preheated bowls. Place a few slices of the cooked chuck and raw sirloin on the noodles. Bring the broth to a rolling boil and ladle 2 to 3 cups of broth into each bowl. The broth will cook the raw beef instantly.

Garnish with scallions, cilantro, sprouts, herbs, chilies, lime juice, and black pepper. Serve immediately.

Pork and Watercress Soup *Serves 4*

2 ounces lean pork
6 cups chicken stock
½ inch fresh ginger,* sliced
1½ tablespoons sherry
½ bunch watercress,* sliced
1 green onion, thinly sliced
Salt to taste

Cut pork across the grain into ¼-inch slices and then into ⅛-inch strips. In a large pot, heat the stock almost to a boil. Add pork strips and ginger. Reduce heat, cover, and simmer until meat is no longer pink, about 10 minutes. Discard ginger slices and skim the soup. Stir in the sherry. Add watercress and green onion. Simmer uncovered until watercress softens, but still retains its fresh green color, about 3 minutes. Season and serve.

Portuguese Bean Soup

An Island favorite.

½ pound dried kidney beans
2 to 3 ham hocks
1½ to 2 pounds hot Portuguese sausage,* cut in ½-inch slices,
    sautéed and drained
1 (8-ounce) can tomato sauce
2 large baking potatoes, cut into ¾-inch cubes
1 onion, sliced
3 carrots, sliced
3 stalks celery, sliced
3 tablespoons minced parsley
1 clove garlic, minced
1 tablespoon lemon juice
½ head medium cabbage, shredded (optional)
½ cup uncooked macaroni (optional)
1 bunch watercress,* chopped (optional)
Salt, pepper and allspice to taste

Cover beans with water and soak overnight. Drain. Cover ham hocks with water and cook for 1 to 1½ hours. Remove ham hocks, shred meat, and discard bone and fat. Add beans to liquid and cook for 1 hour. Return meat to soup along with Portuguese sausage. Cook for 10 minutes. Add tomato sauce, potatoes, onion, carrots, celery, parsley, garlic, and lemon juice. Simmer until vegetables are tender. Add cabbage, macaroni, watercress, salt, pepper, and allspice. Simmer for 10 minutes or until macaroni is tender.

Sausage Minestrone

Great for Monday night football.

½ pound Italian sausage, casing removed
1 cup onion, coarsely chopped
½ cup carrots, peeled and coarsely chopped
½ cup celery, coarsely chopped
4 tablespoons parsley, chopped
2 (14½-ounce) cans Italian-style tomatoes, broken with a fork
2 (14½-ounce) cans chicken broth
1 teaspoon basil
½ cup spaghetti, broken into pieces salt and freshly ground
   pepper to taste
Garnish: freshly grated Parmesan cheese*

In a saucepan, brown the sausage, breaking it up into bite-size pieces as it cooks. Remove sausage, using drippings to sauté the onion until tender. Discard drippings. Add the sausage, vegetables, chicken broth, and basil to the saucepan and bring to a boil. Cook over medium heat for 15 minutes. Add spaghetti pieces, salt and pepper. Reduce heat, cover, and simmer for 20 minutes. Garnish and serve.

Italian Clam Stew

Serves 4 to 6

⅓ cup olive oil*
1 onion, chopped
4 cloves garlic, minced
1 teaspoon or dried basil or 6 leaves fresh basil, minced
1 teaspoon dried oregano
1 (6-ounce) can tomato paste
¼ cup white wine
1½ cups water
Salt and freshly ground pepper to taste
40 littleneck clams, rinsed

Sauté onion and garlic in olive oil until soft and translucent. Add remaining ingredients except for clams and bring to a boil. Season, reduce heat, and simmer for 5 minutes. Add clams, cover, and simmer stirring occasionally until clams open, about 5 to 10 minutes.

Mediterranean Fish Stew   *Serves 6*

2 tablespoons olive oil*
1 large onion, chopped
1 large carrot, peeled and chopped
3 cloves garlic, minced
1 (6-ounce) can tomato paste
¾ cup dry white wine
1 cup water
Salt and freshly ground pepper to taste
2 teaspoons dried basil
½ teaspoon dried red chili pepper
2 pounds firm white fish fillets (turbot, snapper, haddock,
    halibut, sole, orange roughy, etc.)
Garnish: chopped parsley

In a large Dutch oven or flame-proof casserole dish, sauté onion and carrot in oil until tender. Add garlic, tomato paste, wine, water, and seasonings. Cover and simmer for 30 minutes. Preheat oven to 375°F. Arrange fish fillets on top of tomato-vegetable sauce and bake for 20 to 30 minutes. Garnish with parsley.

Corn Chowder

Serves 6

1 pound bacon
3 tablespoons flour
1 cup diced onion
1 cup diced celery
1 cup diced carrots
2 cups diced potatoes
1 quart milk
1 (17-ounce) can cream style corn
2 teaspoons salt
½ teaspoon white pepper
1 teaspoon Worcestershire sauce
Garnish: chopped parsley

Dice and fry the bacon. Pour off all but 2 tablespoons of drippings. Add flour to bacon. Stir and turn off heat. Combine onion, celery, carrots, and potatoes in a saucepan and barely cover with water. Cook for 10 minutes. Add water and vegetables to bacon and cook another 10 minutes. Stir in milk, corn, salt, pepper, and Worcestershire. Bring ingredients to a boil. Garnish and serve.

Variation: 1 cup grated Cheddar cheese or Gruyère cheese may be stirred in before serving.

Albert Schmid
Executive Chef
Dillingham Corporation
Honolulu, Hawai'i

Mahimahi Chowder *Serves 10 to 12*

6 slices bacon, cut into small pieces
2 medium onions, chopped
3 stalks celery, chopped
8 sprigs parsley, chopped
2 potatoes, peeled and diced
½ cup water
12 ounces mahimahi* fillets
¼ teaspoon white pepper
1½ to 2 teaspoons garlic salt
2 cups whipping cream
2½ cups half-and-half
¾ to 1 tablespoon cornstarch
½ ounce dry sherry
Garnish: chopped parsley

Fry bacon in a heavy saucepan. Remove bacon, using drippings to sauté onion, celery, and parsley until tender. Add diced potatoes and water to saucepan. Cover and simmer until potatoes are tender. Stir in bacon. Place fillets on top of soup, cover, and steam* until fish flakes easily. Break into bite-size pieces and stir into soup. Add white pepper and garlic salt. Stir in cream and half-and-half and heat thoroughly. In a separate cup, combine cornstarch and sherry. Slowly stir into chowder to thicken. Heat just to boiling, remove from heat and serve immediately. Garnish with parsley.

Breads

Kahuku Ranch Bread

Makes 2 loaves

This bread is excellent for toasting.

5½ to 6 cups flour
2 packages (2 tablespoons) active dry yeast
1 tablespoon sugar
2 teaspoons salt
¼ teaspoon baking soda
2 cups milk
½ cup water
Corn meal

Combine 3 cups flour yeast, sugar, salt, and baking soda. Heat milk and water until very warm (120 to 130°F) and add to dry ingredients. Beat well. Stir in enough flour to make a stiff batter. Dough is ready to knead when it is stiff enough to pull away from sides of the bowl with a wooden spoon. Turn onto floured board and knead until smooth and elastic. Add more flour if dough is sticky. Divide dough in half and shape into loaves. Place loaves into two 9 x 5 x 3-inch loaf pans which have been oiled and sprinkled with corn meal. Cover and let rise in a warm place until double, about 45 minutes. Preheat oven to 400°F. Bake for 25 minutes. Turn loaves out onto rack to cool.

Blue Ribbon Banana Bread

Makes 2 loaves

3 eggs
½ cup vegetable oil
½ cup butter or margarine, melted
1½ cups sugar
2 cups flour (may use 1 cup whole wheat and
    1 cup all-purpose)
2 teaspoons baking soda
½ teaspoon salt
Pinch cinnamon
2 cups bananas, sliced and firmly packed
1 teaspoon vanilla
2 cups walnuts, chopped

Preheat oven to 350°F. Grease and flour two 8½ x 4½ x 2½-inch loaf pans. Beat eggs, oil, butter, and sugar for 2 minutes. Add dry ingredients and mix well. Add bananas and vanilla and mix until bananas are mashed. Add nuts. Pour into prepared pans and bake for 50 to 55 minutes or until a toothpick comes out clean. Remove from pans immediately and cool on a wire rack.

Note: For terrific mango bread, substitute 2 cups drained mangos for the bananas and add 2 teaspoons cinnamon.

The first Hawaiians brought the Hawaiian banana plant to the islands from the South Pacific. It now grows wild in mountain valleys. Today the most common and most delectable varieties grown in Hawai'i are the Chinese, Bluefield, and the Brazilian Apple bananas. They grow in warm, moist areas and ripen year-round, one bunch to a tree. Bananas are usually eaten raw but also may be cooked ripe or green, as substitute for white or sweet potatoes.

Banana Lemon
Tea Bread

Serves 12 to 14

⅔ cup shortening
1 cup sugar
2 eggs
1½ cups mashed ripe bananas
6 tablespoons lemon juice
2 cups flour
1 teaspoon baking soda
1 teaspoon salt
1 tablespoon grated lemon peel

Preheat oven to 350°F. Grease a Bundt pan or two medium loaf pans. Cream shortening and sugar. Blend in eggs, bananas, and lemon juice. Sift dry ingredients and stir into batter. Add grated lemon peel. Pour into prepared pan and bake for one hour.

Mango Bread

Makes 3 small loaves

Freeze mango purée for use when mangoes are out of season.

2 cups mango* purée (papaya* purée or papaya yogurt may be
    substituted)
1 cup vegetable oil
3 eggs
1 teaspoon vanilla
Grated peel of 1 orange (optional)
2 cups flour (may use 1 cup whole wheat, 1 cup all purpose)
2 teaspoons baking soda
½ teaspoon salt
1½ cups sugar
¼ teaspoon ground cloves
½ teaspoon pumpkin pie spice (optional)
¼ teaspoon nutmeg
2 teaspoons cinnamon
1 cup bran buds or granola
1 cup raisins
1 cup chopped nuts (optional)
½ cup shredded coconut* (optional)

Preheat oven to 350°F. Grease three 3 x 7-inch loaf pans. In
a blender, blend mango purée, oil, eggs, vanilla, and orange
peel. Sift flour, baking powder, and salt. Add sugar and spices.
Combine mango mixture with dry ingredients. Stir in raisins,
nuts, and coconut. Spoon mixture almost to top of pans. Bake
for one hour or until done.

Zucchini Bread

Makes 2 loaves

3 eggs
2 cups sugar
1 cup vegetable oil
2 cups grated raw zucchini
3 teaspoons vanilla
3 cups flour
1 teaspoon salt
1 teaspoon baking soda
¼ teaspoon baking powder
3 teaspoons cinnamon
1 cup chopped walnuts (optional)

Preheat oven to 350°F. Butter 2 one-pound loaf pans. Beat eggs until light and foamy. Add sugar, oil, zucchini, and vanilla. Do not over-mix. Combine dry ingredients and stir into zucchini mixture. Add nuts and pour into pans. Bake for 60 minutes. Cool on wire rack.

Family Pumpkin Bread

Makes two large or three medium loaves

2⅔ cups sugar
⅔ cup shortening
4 eggs
1 pound canned pumpkin
⅔ cup water
3⅓ cups flour
2 teaspoons baking soda
1½ teaspoons salt
½ teaspoon baking powder
1 teaspoon cinnamon
1 teaspoon cloves
⅔ cup walnuts
⅔ cup golden raisins
3 tablespoons powdered sugar

Preheat oven to 350°F. Grease and flour two 9 x 5 x 3-inch (or three 8½ x 4½-inch) loaf pans. Cream sugar and shortening until fluffy. Stir in eggs, pumpkin, and water. Combine dry ingredients and stir into pumpkin mixture. Add walnuts and golden raisins and pour into pans. Bake for 1 hour and 10 minutes or until toothpick inserted in center of loaf comes out clean. Cool on wire rack. Sprinkle top with powdered sugar.

Note: For a cookie bar bake in a 9 x 13-inch pan.

Pineapple Zucchini Loaf

Makes two loaves

3 eggs
2 cups granulated sugar
1 cup vegetable oil
3 tablespoons vanilla
2 cups grated fresh zucchini, with or without peel,
    well-drained
3 cups all-purpose flour
1 teaspoon baking powder
1 teaspoon baking soda
1 teaspoon salt
1 teaspoon ground cardamom
8 ounces crushed pineapple,* drained
1 cup chopped pecans, walnuts or macadamia nuts*
½ cup raisins

Heat oven to 350°F. Grease and flour two 9 x 5-inch loaf pans. Set aside. In a large bowl, beat eggs until light and fluffy. Add sugar, oil, and vanilla. Blend well. Stir in zucchini, mixing thoroughly. Sift in flour, baking powder, baking soda, salt, and cardamom. Stir to blend. Add pineapple, nuts, and raisins. Mix well. Pour into prepared pans.

Bake for 60 minutes or until a cake tester inserted in the center of the loaves comes out clean. Cool on wire rack about 10 minutes before removing from pans. Cool completely. Store wrapped tightly in plastic wrap.

Note: This bread gets better the next day as the flavors have time to develop overnight.

Pineapple-Coconut Bread

Makes one loaf

½ cup warm water (105°F to 115°F)
¼ cup warm milk (105°F to 115°F)
2 tablespoons honey
1 package yeast
2 tablespoons butter softened
¼ teaspoon ground ginger*
¼ teaspoon ground nutmeg
½ teaspoon salt
½ cup whole wheat flour
2 cups all-purpose flour
¼ cup finely diced dried pineapple*
¼ cup shredded coconut*
¼ cup diced macadamia nuts*

Mix water, milk, and honey in a large bowl. Sprinkle in yeast and let stand to proof about 5 minutes. Add butter, ginger, nutmeg, salt, and whole wheat flour, stirring to blend. Add all-purpose flour a ½ cup at a time, mixing well after each addition, until dough pulls away from side of bowl. Knead dough by hand or electric stand mixer, adding more flour as necessary, until smooth and elastic. Place in a lightly oiled bowl, turning to coat lightly. Cover with a clean cloth and let rise in a warm, draft free place for 1 hour.

Punch dough down. Add pineapple, coconut, and macadamia nuts. Knead 5 minutes to incorporate well. Grease and flour an 8-inch loaf pan. Shape dough into loaf and fit into pan. Cover and let rise for 45 minutes. Heat oven to 400°F. Place bread in center of oven and bake 35 to 40 minutes until top is crusty, bottom is browned and sounds hollow when tapped. Let bread rest in pan for 5 minutes on wire rack before removing from pan to wire rack to cool completely. Store wrapped tightly in plastic wrap.

Feather-Weight Coffee Cake

A light and easy coffee cake.

4 teaspoons butter or margarine, melted
1 egg, beaten
½ cup milk
1 cup flour
¾ cup sugar, divided
3 teaspoons baking powder
½ teaspoon salt
¼ cup sugar
1 teaspoon cinnamon

Preheat oven to 375°F. Grease an 8-inch square pan. Mix butter, egg, and milk in a small bowl. Combine flour, ½ cup sugar, baking powder, and salt and sift 3 times. Add dry ingredients to milk mixture and mix together just enough to combine smoothly. Pour into prepared pan. Combine ¼ cup sugar and cinnamon and sprinkle over cake. Bake for 12 to 15 minutes. Serve immediately as is or with butter and jelly.

Tūtū's Kuchen

Grandmother's delicious holiday coffee cake.

1 cup milk, scalded and cooled to lukewarm
1 package (1 tablespoon) active dry yeast
4 tablespoons shortening
2 tablespoons sugar
2 eggs, beaten
½ teaspoon salt
3¼ cups sifted flour
4 tablespoons melted butter
½ cup sugar
2 teaspoons cinnamon
Candied fruit, crushed pineapple,* chopped nuts, raisins

Grease a 10-inch tube pan. Add yeast to lukewarm milk, stirring until dissolved. In a mixing bowl, cream shortening and sugar. Add eggs, cooled milk, salt, and flour, blending well. Place bowl in a warm place and let rise until doubled in size. Punch down. Pinch off pieces of dough and form walnut-sized balls. Dip balls into melted butter, then roll thoroughly in sugar and cinnamon mixture. Layer balls in pan, sprinkling fruits and nuts throughout. Let rise 1 hour. Preheat oven to 350°F. Bake for 30 to 40 minutes. Cool for a few minutes before turning out on a serving platter. To serve, pull apart.

Cinnamon Swirl Raisin Bread

Makes 2 loaves

8 cups flour
1 package (1 tablespoon) active dry yeast
2 cups milk
¼ cup sugar
¼ cup butter
2 teaspoons salt
3 eggs
½ cup sugar
2 teaspoons ground cinnamon
2 cups raisins, soaked until softened

Combine 3 cups flour and yeast in a large bowl.

In a saucepan, heat milk, sugar, butter, and salt until warm (115°F-120°F) and butter is almost melted, stirring constantly. Add to flour mixture and add eggs. Beat at low speed of electric mixer ½ minute, scraping bowl. Beat at high speed until smooth, about 3 minutes. Mix in enough of the remaining flour to make dough stiff enough to pull away from the sides of the bowl with a wooden spoon. Stir in raisins.

Turn out onto a lightly floured surface. Knead until dough is smooth and elastic, about 6 to 8 minutes. Add remaining flour as necessary. Shape into a ball. Place in a lightly greased bowl and turn once to grease top. Cover loosely with clear plastic wrap or a damp cloth. Let rise in a warm place until doubled (about 1¼ hours).

Punch down dough. Divide dough in half. Cover and let rest for 10 minutes. Roll each half of the dough on a lightly floured surface into 15 x 7-inch rectangle. Brush dough lightly with water. Combine sugar and cinnamon and sprinkle over dough.

Beginning with the narrow end, roll up tightly. Pinch edge of dough into roll to seal well. Press each end with side of hand to seal and fold ends under. Place loaves seam sides down in 2 greased 9 x 5 x 3-inch loaf pans. Cover and let rise until nearly double, about 35 to 45 minutes.

Preheat oven to 375°F. Bake for 35 to 45 minutes, covering with foil during last 15 minutes to prevent over-browning. Remove from pans and cool on a wire rack. Drizzle with icing.

Icing
1 cup powdered sugar, sifted
¼ teaspoon vanilla
1 teaspoon milk

Combine powdered sugar vanilla and milk. Blend until smooth.

Longhi's Cinnamon Rolls

Makes 18 to 20 rolls

½ cup warm water
1 package (1 tablespoon) active dry yeast
3 tablespoons sugar
⅔ cup milk, scalded and cooled
¼ cup melted butter
2 eggs
½ teaspoon salt
2½ cups flour
2 cups whole wheat flour
¼ cup melted butter
½ cup raisins, soaked in water until softened
⅔ cup brown sugar, firmly packed
1½ tablespoons cinnamon
½ to ¾ cup chopped pecans (optional)

Combine water and yeast, stirring until dissolved. Add sugar and let stand 15 to 20 minutes or until yeast begins to bubble.

Combine yeast mixture, milk, butter, eggs, and salt in a large bowl and mix well. Add flour to make a stiff dough. Cover and let rise until doubled.

Punch down dough. Roll dough on lightly floured surface into 23 x 14-inch rectangle. Brush with melted butter and sprinkle with raisins. Combine brown sugar, cinnamon, and pecans and sprinkle over dough. Roll into cylinder shape as for jelly roll. Slice dough into 1 to 1½ inch strips. Place rolls flat on greased baking sheets or in three 8-inch square pans. Cover and let rise in warm place until double in size, approximately 30 to 45 minutes.

Preheat oven to 350°F. Bake for 20 to 25 minutes. Brush with butter and drizzle with icing.

Icing
1½ to 2 cups powdered sugar
2 tablespoons light corn syrup
Juice of 1 orange or lemon

Combine powdered sugar, corn syrup, and juice. Blend until smooth.

Longhi's Restaurant
Lahaina, Maui

Coconut Cinnamon Sour Cream Coffee Cake

Serves 10 to 12

1 cup butter
2 cups sugar
2 cups flour
¼ teaspoon salt
1 teaspoon baking powder
3 eggs
1 teaspoon vanilla
1 cup sour cream
1½ cups flaked coconut*

Spice filling
1 cup chopped pecans
3 to 4 teaspoons cinnamon
6 tablespoons brown sugar
½ to ¾ cup flaked coconut*

Preheat oven to 325°F. Grease Bundt pan. Cream butter and sugar. Sift dry ingredients and add to creamed mixture, alternating with eggs. Stir in vanilla, sour cream, and coconut. In a separate bowl, combine filling ingredients. Pour half of the batter into Bundt pan, then add half of the filling mixture. Add remaining batter and sprinkle balance of filling on top. Bake for 1¼ to 1½ hours.

Green Tea Bread
with Candied Ginger

2 cups all-purpose flour
2 teaspoons ground ginger*
1 teaspoon baking powder
1 teaspoon salt
¼ teaspoon baking soda
¼ cup loose green tea leaves, finely ground
¼ cup finely chopped candied ginger*
Grated zest of 1 lemon
4 eggs
1 cup granulated sugar
¾ cup mild olive oil*
2 tablespoons fresh lemon juice
2 teaspoons vanilla extract

Position a baking rack in the lower third of the oven. Heat oven to 350°F. Lightly oil a 9 x 5-inch loaf pan and line with parchment or waxed paper. In a medium bowl, sift together flour, ginger, baking powder, salt, and baking soda. Stir in green tea, candied ginger, and lemon zest. Set aside.

Break eggs into a large bowl. Beat 2 minutes until light in color and frothy. Slowly add the sugar in three stages, beating 30 seconds between each addition. Combine oil, lemon juice, and vanilla in measuring cup. Drizzle into egg mixture while beating. Stir in dry ingredients all at once mixing just until blended. Scrape batter into prepared pan.

Bake 50 to 55 minutes until a knife inserted in the center of the loaf comes out clean. Remove from oven and let bread cool at least 30 minutes on cooling rack. Remove from pan and cool completely. Store wrapped tightly in plastic wrap.

Sweet Cornbread

The sugar adds a hint of sweetness to this bread.

½ cup butter
1 cup sugar
2 eggs
2 cups flour
6 tablespoons cornmeal
3 teaspoons baking powder
½ teaspoon salt
¼ teaspoon baking soda
1 cup milk

Preheat oven to 350°F. Grease a 9 x 13-inch baking pan. Cream butter and sugar until fluffy. Blend in eggs.

Combine dry ingredients and stir into creamed mixture. Add milk and mix well. Pour into prepared pan. Bake for 30 to 35 minutes. While cornbread is still warm, spread top generously with soft butter.

Dutch Baby

This fluffy oven pancake cooks in a large frying pan.

¼ cup butter
3 eggs
¾ cup milk
¾ cup flour

Preheat oven to 425°F. Melt butter in a 2- to 3-quart frying pan or shallow baking dish. Whirl eggs for one minute in blender, gradually adding milk and flour. Pour batter into hot buttered pan and bake for 20 to 25 minutes. Serve immediately with your choice of toppings: powdered sugar and lemon juice, honey, syrup, jams and jellies, fresh fruit, or heated fruits.

Note: This recipe doubles well. Use a 5-quart pan.

Kahala Challah

Makes two loaves

2 packages active dry yeast
1 cup warm water (105°F to 115°F)
½ cup granulated sugar divided
4 eggs
5 cups all-purpose flour
2 teaspoons salt
½ cup butter softened
1 tablespoon poppy seeds

In a large bowl, dissolve yeast in warm water with a few tablespoons of sugar and let stand until foamy, about 5 to 10 minutes. With wooden spoon, stir in remaining sugar and 3 eggs, blending well. Add 4½ cups flour, salt, and butter, stirring until mixture comes together to form a sticky dough. Knead dough by hand or electric stand mixer about 8 minutes, adding very little flour, until smooth and elastic. Be careful not to add too much flour. The dough should stay soft and will become less sticky with kneading. Form into a ball. Place in a lightly oiled bowl, turning to coat. Cover with a clean, damp cloth and let rise in a warm, draft free place until double in bulk, about 2 hours.

Oil baking sheet or line with parchment paper. Set aside. Punch dough down. Scrape out onto floured work surface. Divide dough in half. Cut each half into three equal pieces. Gently roll each piece by starting in center of dough and working outward to form a 12-inch rope. Line up the three pieces vertically. Starting at the top, braid ropes by crossing the strand on the right over the middle strand, then the left strand over the new middle piece. Repeat until all of the ropes have been incorporated into the braid. Pinch the ends together and tuck under. Tidy up the top by crossing any loose ends under each other, pinching together, and tucking under the loaf.

Place braided loaves on prepared baking sheet, cover with a dry cloth, and let rise in a warm place until double in size and spongy to touch, about 1 hour.

Position rack in lower third of oven and heat to 350°F. Beat remaining egg and brush over the top of the bread. Sprinkle with poppy seeds. Bake for 30 to 35 minutes until nicely browned and loaves sound hollow when tapped on bottom. Transfer to wire rack to cool.

This recipe can be cut in half for just one loaf. Break eggs into a cup, beat until smooth, and reserve 1 to 2 tablespoons for egg wash.

Note: Yeast is a living organism that needs food, warmth, and moisture to thrive. Proofing or activating the yeast before adding it is one step to take in assuring the success of the bread. High heat can kill it and not enough heat will slow it down.

Maui Onion Focaccia

Makes one loaf

1 package dry yeast
½ teaspoon granulated sugar
1 cup warm water (105°F to 115°F), divided
3 cups all-purpose flour
1 teaspoon salt
4 tablespoons olive oil,* divided
2 Maui or 'Ewa Sweet onions, diced or thinly sliced
8 cloves garlic, minced
1 tablespoon fresh chopped rosemary or basil
Parmesan or chopped walnuts

In a large bowl, dissolve yeast and sugar in ¼ cup warm water. Let sit 5 to 10 minutes until foamy.

Add remaining ¾ cup of water, flour, salt, and 1 tablespoon of oil, stirring to make a soft dough. Turn out onto floured surface. Knead dough for 8 to 10 minutes. Let rest for 2 or 3 minutes. Knead another 5 minutes until dough is very smooth and elastic. Place in a lightly oiled bowl, turning to coat lightly. Cover and let rise in a warm place until double in bulk, about 1½ hours.

Punch dough down. Lightly oil a 12 x 16-inch pan with slight rim. Place dough on pan and press evenly to reach edges. Set aside.

Heat remaining oil in a medium skillet over medium-high heat. Add onion, garlic, and herbs. Sauté until golden, 8 to 10 minutes.

Dimple dough by poking with finger. Spread with sautéed onions. Let rise uncovered in a warm place for 30 minutes.

Heat oven to 400°F. Sprinkle focaccia with cheese or walnuts. Bake in the middle of the oven about 25 minutes until golden and bottom is lightly browned. Remove to wire rack and let sit a few minutes before cutting into squares or on diagonal for diamonds. Serve warm.

Note: This can be frozen. Thaw at room temperature and bake at 350°F just until heated through, about 10 minutes.

Onion varieties include yellow, white, Spanish, red, or Bermuda; and sweet onions, such as Vidalia, Maui, and Walla Walla named after the locations in which they're grown. The true Maui onion grows in the deep red, volcanic earth on the upper slopes of Haleakalā, on the island of Maui, and is considered one of the best and most flavorful onions in the world.

Portuguese Malasadas

Malasadas* are traditionally eaten on Shrove Tuesday, before the start of Lent.

2½ teaspoons active dry yeast
1 teaspoon sugar
⅓ cup warm water
6 cups flour
1 cup sugar
1 teaspoon salt
1 cup milk
1 potato, cooked and mashed
⅔ cup water
⅓ cup butter, melted
5 eggs, beaten
Vegetable oil for deep frying sugar

Mix yeast with 1 teaspoon sugar and add to warm water. Let stand for 5 minutes. Mix flour, sugar, and salt in a large bowl. Stir in milk, potato, and water. Add butter, eggs, and yeast mixture and mix well. Cover and let dough rise for 2 hours in a warm spot. Heat 2 to 3 inches of oil in a deep fryer to 375°F. Dip fingertips in bowl of oil or softened butter then pinch off golf ball-size pieces of raised dough. Drop in heated oil and cook until golden brown on one side. Turn over and fry until golden brown on the other side. Drain on paper towels and roll in sugar. Serve immediately.

Punahou Malasadas

Makes 5 dozen

At their carnival, Punahou School sells 85,000 malasadas* in just two days.

  1 package (1 tablespoon) active dry yeast
  1 teaspoon sugar
  ¼ cup warm water
  6 cups flour
  ½ cup sugar
  ½ teaspoon salt
  ¼ cup melted butter
  6 eggs
  1 cup evaporated milk
  1 cup water
  Vegetable oil for deep frying
  Sugar and dash of nutmeg

Mix yeast with 1 teaspoon sugar and add to warm water. Let stand for 5 minutes. Sift dry ingredients together. Stir in melted butter. Beat eggs, milk, and water together and add to flour mixture. Add yeast and mix well. Dough will be sticky. Cover and let dough rise until doubled, then punch down. Let dough rise a second time. Heat oil in deep fryer to 375°F. Dip fingertips in bowl or oil or softened butter then pinch off golf ball size pieces of raised dough. Drop in heated oil and cook until golden brown on one side. Turn over and fry until golden on the other side. Drain on paper towels and roll in sugar-nutmeg mixture. Serve immediately.

Note: This recipe doubles well.

Lavosh

2¾ cups flour
½ teaspoon baking soda
½ teaspoon salt
¼ cup sugar
½ cup butter
1 cup buttermilk
Lightly toasted sesame seeds*
Poppy seeds

Preheat oven to 375°F. Lightly grease a cookie sheet. Sift dry ingredients together. Cut in butter. Add buttermilk and mix until batter forms a big ball. Pinch off tablespoon-size balls of dough. Flour a cutting board and sprinkle with sesame and poppy seeds. Roll out each ball of dough until it is quite thin. Pick up rolled dough on rolling pin and place on cookie sheet. Repeat process of flouring the cutting board and sprinkling with seeds as needed. Bake each batch for 6 to 8 minutes or until golden brown.

Entrées

Meats

Poultry

Thai Beef Salad

⅓ cup fresh lime juice
2 tablespoons packed brown sugar
1 tablespoon water
1 tablespoon fish sauce*
2 to 4 cloves garlic, minced
¼ teaspoon chili paste
1 stalk lemongrass

Salad
1 pound flank steak
Salt and black pepper
1 head romaine lettuce
1 pint cherry tomatoes halved
1 medium red onion, thinly sliced
¼ cup coarsely chopped fresh mint
¼ cup chopped cilantro*

Combine lime juice, sugar, water, fish sauce, garlic, and chili paste in a bowl with a whisk, blending well. Thinly slice lemongrass and stir into dressing. Set aside.

Prepare grill or broiler. Sprinkle both sides of steak with a little salt and pepper. Place on hot grill rack. Cook 6 minutes per side. Remove from heat and let stand 10 minutes.

Wash and pat dry lettuce. Tear into bite-sized pieces. Place in a large salad bowl. Add tomatoes. Separate onion slices into rings and scatter across salad. Cut steak diagonally across the grain into thin slices. Cut slices into 2-inch pieces and add to salad. Sprinkle with mint and cilantro. Add dressing, toss to coat, and serve.

To make ahead, prepare dressing; cook and slice meat; wash and pat dry lettuce; halve tomatoes; slice onion; chop herbs; but store everything separately. Assemble just before serving.

Classical Korean Dried Beef

Serves 8 to 10

This dish is usually garnished with dried cuttlefish, cut in artistic shapes.

> 1 pound beef round steak
> 4 tablespoons soy sauce*
> 2 teaspoons dry white wine
> 1 tablespoon sugar
> 1 teaspoon garlic juice
> ⅛ teaspoon fresh ginger* juice
> ¼ teaspoon pepper
> 2 tablespoons peanut oil*
> 1 teaspoon sesame oil*
> Garnish: pine nuts and dried cuttlefish*

Slice beef across grain into ⅛-inch strips and place in a bowl. Combine soy sauce, wine, sugar, garlic juice, ginger juice, and pepper. Add to meat. Spread beef slices on a wire rack and dry in the sun. Turn often until dried. (Meat will take 1 to 3 days to dry.) For a richer color, brush a combination of peanut and sesame oil lightly over the meat slices. When dried, broil over charcoal and cut into serving pieces. Serve on a platter and garnish with nuts and dried cuttlefish.

Note: Dried cuttlefish can easily be carved into shapes such as flowers and birds.

Hot Mongolian Beef

Serves 4

½ pound flank steak
1 egg
1 tablespoon water
1 tablespoon cornstarch
5 cups vegetable oil
¼ ounce long rice*
¼ pound carrot, shredded
¼ pound bell pepper, shredded
3 cloves garlic, minced
1 teaspoon minced fresh ginger*
6 to 7 Hawaiian chili peppers*
1 teaspoon cooking wine
1 tablespoon soy sauce*
1 teaspoon sugar

Thinly slice beef. Combine egg, water, and cornstarch.

Add beef, stir and let stand for 2 hours. Heat wok* until hot. Add oil and let stand for 10 seconds. Deep fry long rice to puff and place on platter. Put beef into wok. Separate beef with a ladle until half-cooked. Add carrot and bell pepper. Stir until oil starts boiling. Drain, reserve leftover oil. Add garlic, ginger, chili peppers, wine, soy sauce, and sugar. Stir 5 seconds, put drained beef into wok, stir and flip several times. Serve over crispy long rice.

Howard Co
Yen King Restaurant
Honolulu, Hawaii

Oven-Barbecued Spareribs   *Serves 6*

A staple of Island picnics.

    3 to 4 pounds pork spare ribs
    ¾ cup brown sugar
    ½ cup cider vinegar
    ¼ cup soy sauce*
    3 tablespoons dry mustard
    8 to 10 dashes Tabasco
    ¾ teaspoon garlic salt

Bring spareribs to a boil in salted water and cover. Reduce heat and simmer until meat is tender, approximately 1 hour. Preheat oven to 325°F. Combine brown sugar, vinegar, soy sauce, mustard, Tabasco, and garlic salt and heat to boiling. Drain spareribs and arrange meaty sides up on rack in shallow roasting pan. Spread with marinade and roast, basting frequently, until done and glazed, about 1 hour.

Pulehu Ribs   *Serves 4*

Pulehu means "to broil" in Hawaiian.

    3 pounds beef short ribs
    1 tablespoon sugar
    1 tablespoon Hawaiian rock salt*
    1½ tablespoons soy sauce*
    1½ teaspoons Chili Pepper Water* (see page 178)
    1 teaspoon sesame oil*

Combine ingredients and rub into ribs. Let stand for 3 to 4 hours. Grill over charcoal.

Short Ribs

5 pounds beef or pork short ribs
½ cup all-purpose flour
2 teaspoons salt
½ to 1 teaspoon black pepper
2 large onions, thinly sliced
¾ cup catsup
2 tablespoons vinegar
2 tablespoons Worcestershire sauce
4 tablespoons soy sauce*
½ cup granulated or packed brown sugar
¾ cup water

Heat oven to 350°F. Cut ribs into 3 to 5-inch pieces. Mix flour, salt, and pepper in a shallow dish. Roll ribs in seasoned flour. Arrange in a large roasting pan. Spread onion slices over ribs. In a bowl, whisk together catsup, vinegar, Worcestershire, soy sauce, sugar, and water. Pour over ribs. Cover with foil and bake for 3 hours until tender. Remove foil the last 30 minutes to brown meat. Remove from oven. Place on serving platter with sauce. Serve.

Note: Great with steamed rice.

Kalbi   *Serves 4*

Distinctly Korean, these ribs are a popular barbecue entrée.

    2 to 3 pounds beef short ribs
    ¾ cup soy sauce*
    ¾ cup sugar
    ¾ cup water
    3-inch piece fresh ginger* sliced
    1 clove garlic, minced
    1 tablespoon sesame oil*

Combine ingredients and marinate ribs for 4 hours. Broil or barbecue.

Four Peppercorn Pork Roast

Serves 8 to 10

4½ pound boneless pork loin, tied
3 tablespoons unsalted butter, softened
2 tablespoons flour
¼ cup mixed peppercorns, very coarsely crushed
¼ cup flour
1¾ cups chicken broth
1 cup water
2 tablespoons red wine vinegar*
Salt to taste
Garnish: fresh rosemary

Preheat oven to 475°F. Season roast with salt. Combine the butter and 2 tablespoons of flour to make a paste. Spread the top of the roast with the paste. Lightly press the peppercorns into the butter paste. Place the pork on a rack in a roasting pan. Roast at 475°F for 30 minutes. Reduce heat to 325°F and continue roasting for 1½ to 1⅔ hours or until meat thermometer registers 155°F. Transfer the roast to cutting board and let stand for 10 minutes.

Prepare sauce while the roast is standing. Pour all but ¼ cup of fat from the roasting pan. Whisk in flour and cook over moderate heat for 3 minutes, stirring constantly. Slowly stir in the chicken broth and water. Bring to a boil. Stir in red wine vinegar and salt to taste. Simmer sauce until thickened to desired consistency. Remove string from roast and cut into ½-inch thick slices. Arrange on platter with sauce and garnish with fresh rosemary.

Hoisin Pork with Pineapple Relish

Serves 4

Pineapple Relish
2 cups fresh or canned pineapple* tidbits, well-drained
1 jalapeño pepper minced
1 tablespoon lime juice
1 tablespoon honey
1 tablespoon olive oil*
3 green onions, thinly sliced
2 tablespoons chopped cilantro*
Salt and black pepper

Sandwich
½ cup hoisin sauce*
1 tablespoon apple cider vinegar
1 tablespoon soy sauce*
2 cloves garlic, crushed
1 teaspoon sesame oil*
8 thin boneless pork chops
4 pita pocket breads, cut in half

Stir together pineapple, jalapeño, lime juice, honey, olive oil, green onion, and cilantro in a non-reactive bowl. Season with salt and pepper to taste. Cover and set aside.

In a small bowl combine hoisin, vinegar, soy sauce, garlic, and sesame oil. Place pork chops in self-sealing bag. Pour hoisin mixture over pork, seal bag, and toss gently to coat well. Set aside for 30 minutes.

Prepare medium-high fire in grill. Remove chops from bag and discard any remaining marinade. Grill pork directly over fire for about 2 minutes per side, until nicely browned. Lightly toast pita bread. Gently open pita pocket and insert grilled chop. Drain any excess liquid from pineapple relish and place spoonfuls over chop. Serve.

Note: Aluminum, unlined copper, and cast iron by themselves react poorly with acidic ingredients such as tomatoes, citrus juice, wine, and vinegar by imparting a metallic taste and an off color. It is extremely important to use non-reactive substances such as stainless steel and glass when cooking or preparing acidic foods.

Smoked Brisket

Serves 6 to 8

Excellent with potato salad and baked beans. Reheat the next day with barbecue sauce for a change of flavor.

3 to 5 pounds beef brisket
1 (3½ ounces) bottle liquid smoke
1 teaspoon garlic salt
1½ teaspoons Beau Monde
¾ teaspoon black pepper
½ teaspoon onion salt
2 teaspoons Worcestershire sauce

Preheat oven to 275°F. Place brisket on a large piece of heavy duty foil. Add seasonings and wrap foil tightly around brisket. Place on rimmed baking sheet and bake for 4 to 5 hours. To serve, slice against the grain or shred.

Vietnamese Style Grilled Pork

¼ cup granulated, sugar
1 cup water divided
2 large shallots, minced
2 tablespoons vegetable oil
2 teaspoons Nuoc Nam (fish sauce*)
2 teaspoons soy sauce*
Pinch salt
2½ pound pork loin, cut into ¼-inch thick slices

In a small saucepan, bring sugar and ½ cup water to a boil over medium heat, stirring occasionally. Reduce heat and simmer, stirring occasionally, until the sauce turns deep brown, about 15 minutes. Meanwhile, heat remaining ½ cup water in a small pan over high heat and bring to a boil, reduce heat to low and keep hot. When sauce reaches the desired color, stir in 4 to 5 tablespoons of hot water carefully as the hot caramel may splatter. Add enough water to make sauce thick enough to coat the back of a spoon. Set caramel sauce aside to cool.

Combine shallots, oil, fish sauce, soy sauce, salt, and caramel sauce, stirring to blend. Add pork loin to sauce. Cover and marinate 20 minutes. Heat grill or broiler. Place pork on grill and cook just until done, about 2 minutes on each side. Arrange on serving platter. Serve.

Note: The caramel is the secret to this dish.

Rosemary Lamb Chops *Serves 4*

Lamb Chops
½ teaspoon white pepper
2 cloves garlic, passed through press
2 teaspoon minced fresh rosemary
8 bone-in lamb loin chops

Cherry Sauce
1 teaspoon olive oil*
1 tablespoon butter
2 large shallots, minced
2 cloves garlic, minced
1 teaspoon grated fresh ginger* root
1 teaspoon minced fresh rosemary
¼ teaspoon salt
½ teaspoon white pepper
1 cup cherry jam
½ cup chopped dried cherries
2 tablespoons balsamic vinegar*

In a small bowl, combine pepper, garlic, and rosemary. Rub over lamb chops. Cover and chill up to 8 hours.

In a small saucepan, heat oil and butter over medium heat. Add shallots, garlic, ginger, and rosemary and sauté until shallots are tender. Stir in salt, pepper, jam, cherries, and vinegar. Heat through. Set aside.

Heat grill. Add meat and cook 6 to 8 minutes per side, to desired doneness. Place on serving platter. Top with a little Cherry Sauce. Serve with additional sauce on the side.

Note: Fresh cherries can be used in the sauce when in season.

Veal Marsala

7 ounces beef broth
4 (1-ounce) boneless veal cutlets
Flour
¼ cup mushrooms, sliced
2 ounces butter
1 ounce Marsala wine
Salt and freshly ground pepper to taste
6 ounces pasta, cooked
Garnish: chopped parsley

Cook beef broth over medium-high heat until reduced by half, stirring constantly. Set aside. Place the veal between two pieces of waxed paper and flatten each cutlet with the flat side of a mallet until thin. Dust lightly in flour. Sauté in butter until slightly browned on all sides. Remove veal. Add the mushrooms and sauté for 1 minute. Add wine and simmer for 1 minute. Add beef broth, salt, and pepper and simmer for 1 minute more. Return veal to pan and cook until heated through. Place veal on top of pasta. Spoon sauce over veal and garnish with chopped parsley.

Miso Chicken

Chicken fillets done Japanese style.

 6 pounds boneless chicken breasts
 ½ cup prepared red miso* or ½ cup white miso* with ½ tea-
     spoon sugar and 2 teaspoons mirin*
 3 stalks green onion, sliced diagonally
 1½ teaspoons toasted sesame seeds*
 ¼ cup shredded pickled red ginger*

Marinate the chicken in the miso for ½ hour. Broil chicken on both sides for 3 minutes, being careful not to overcook. Slice chicken and top with onion, sesame seeds, and ginger.

Lemon Chicken

Serves 6

A Chinese favorite.

3 pounds boneless chicken breasts
1 tablespoon sherry
1 tablespoon soy sauce*
½ teaspoon salt
2 eggs
¼ cup cornstarch
½ teaspoon baking powder
2 cups vegetable oil
⅓ cup sugar
1 tablespoon cornstarch
1 cup chicken broth
1 tablespoon lemon juice
1 teaspoon salt
2 tablespoons vegetable oil
1 lemon, thinly sliced

Combine chicken with sherry, soy sauce, and salt. Marinate for 15 minutes. Beat eggs, cornstarch, and baking powder to form a smooth batter. Heat oil to 350°F. Coat chicken with batter and fry until brown. Cut into 1 x 1½-inch pieces and arrange on a serving dish. Combine sugar, 1 tablespoon cornstarch, broth, lemon juice, and salt. Heat remaining oil. Stir-fry the lemon slices for 30 seconds. Slowly stir in cornstarch mixture. Cook, stirring constantly, until sauce is clear. Pour over chicken and serve immediately.

Orange Chicken Almondine

Serves 6

1 cup dry bread crumbs
¼ cup almonds, finely chopped
1 teaspoon salt
⅛ teaspoon white pepper
2 tablespoons fresh parsley, chopped
¼ cup frozen orange juice concentrate, thawed
¼ cup butter, melted
6 chicken breasts

Preheat oven to 350°F. Combine bread crumbs, almonds, salt, pepper and parsley. Combine orange juice concentrate and butter. Dip chicken breasts into orange juice and butter mixture and then into bread-crumb mixture. Bake in a shallow baking dish for 45 to 50 minutes.

Poulet Dijon

3 pounds boneless chicken breasts, skinned
3 tablespoons butter
2 tablespoons flour
1 cup chicken broth
½ cup half-and-half
2 tablespoons Dijon mustard*
¼ teaspoon salt
¼ teaspoon white pepper
Garnish: tomato wedges and parsley

Sauté chicken in butter over medium heat for 12 to 15 minutes. Transfer chicken to a plate and keep warm. Stir flour into pan drippings. Slowly add broth and cream, stirring until mixture bubbles and thickens. Stir in mustard, salt, and pepper. Pour sauce over chicken and garnish with tomato wedges and parsley.

Steamed Chicken with Lup Cheong

Serves 6

6 to 7 dried black Chinese mushrooms*
1½ teaspoons sugar
3 tablespoons soy sauce*
2 tablespoons water
2 to 3 Lup Cheong sausages,* cut diagonally
3 pounds boneless chicken, skinned and cut in 1-inch pieces
1 tablespoon hoisin sauce*
2 cloves garlic, minced
1 tablespoon bourbon
1 tablespoon chopped green onion
1 tablespoon minced fresh ginger*
1½ tablespoons cornstarch
Garnish: chopped green onion

Soak mushrooms in warm water for 20 minutes. Drain and remove tough stems. Slice into strips. In a skillet, combine sugar, soy sauce, and water. Add sausages and simmer for 10 minutes. In a bowl, combine remaining ingredients. Add simmered mixture and marinate for ½ hour. Steam* covered, for ½ hour or until done. Garnish.

Spicy Eggplant with Chicken

Serves 4

An interesting combination of Asian flavors.

1 teaspoon fresh ginger,* minced
3 tablespoons soy sauce*
1 tablespoon white vinegar
2 to 3 cloves garlic, minced
1 tablespoon sugar
2 to 3 fresh Hawaiian red chili peppers,* minced with seeds
1 teaspoon cornstarch
½ to ¾ pounds long eggplant, sliced diagonally in ½-inch pieces
¾ pound ground chicken or turkey
Vegetable oil
Garnish: Chinese parsley*

Mix ginger, soy sauce, vinegar, garlic, sugar, chili pepper, and cornstarch. Set aside. Sauté eggplant in oil in a large skillet until slices are slightly browned. Set aside. Sauté chicken until browned. Return eggplant to skillet and add sauce. Cook until thoroughly heated. Garnish with Chinese parsley.

Evil Jungle Prince   *Serves 2*

3 to 4 tablespoons dried red curry stock*
¼ cup vegetable oil
½ cup coconut milk*
½ pound sliced boneless chicken breast, skinned
10 to 15 fresh basil leaves
4 tablespoons Thai fish sauce*
½ cup chopped white cabbage

Sauté the dried red curry stock in heated vegetable oil for 3 minutes. Add coconut milk and cook for 2 minutes on medium heat. Add chicken. Cook for 5 minutes. Lower heat to medium low, add basil and fish sauce and serve on a bed of chopped cabbage.

Note: Coconut milk will separate if allowed to come to a boil.

Keo Sananikone
Keo's
Honolulu, Hawai'i

Hawaiian Chicken Curry

Serves 4

1 small onion, finely chopped
1 clove garlic, minced
1 teaspoon fresh ginger,* minced
7 tablespoons butter, divided
1 tablespoon curry powder
1 teaspoon sugar
½ teaspoon salt
3 cups coconut milk*
¼ cup flour
1½ pounds boneless chicken, cut into bite-size pieces

Sauté onion, garlic, and ginger in 2 tablespoons of butter until onion is translucent. Stir in curry powder, sugar, and salt and blend well. Slowly pour in coconut milk, stirring constantly. Reduce heat and simmer for 20 minutes. Strain. Melt 4 tablespoons of butter in a skillet. Stir in flour to make a smooth paste. Add curry sauce and bring to a low boil, stirring constantly. Cook until thickened. Heat remaining tablespoon butter in another skillet and sauté chicken until brown. Add curry sauce and cook until heated through. Serve with fluffy white rice and assorted condiments from the following list.

Curry Condiments:

Chopped bananas
Chutney*
Grated hard-cooked eggs
Chopped green onions
Shredded coconut*
Raisins
Chopped bacon

Diced avocado
Chopped green bell pepper
Diced tomatoes
Black olives
Plain yogurt
Chopped macadamia nuts*
Chopped cucumbers

Chicken Siu Mai

A steamed Chinese dumpling often served as dim sum. *

Dipping Sauce:
1 tablespoon dry hot mustard
½ teaspoon water
⅓ cup soy sauce*

Mix dry mustard with water to form a thick paste. Let stand 15 minutes. Stir in soy sauce. Set aside.

4 shiitake mushrooms*
¼ cup water chestnuts,* chopped
1 tablespoon green onions, chopped
1 pound boneless chicken breast, finely chopped
6 large raw shrimp, cleaned and finely chopped
1¼ teaspoons cornstarch
1½ teaspoons sugar
¼ teaspoon white pepper
1 tablespoon sesame oil*
2 teaspoons soy sauce*
1 tablespoon oyster sauce*
1 egg, beaten
1 (8-ounce) package won ton* wrappers
Lettuce leaves

Soak mushrooms in water for about 30 minutes. Remove stems and discard. Finely chop remainder of mushrooms. Combine mushrooms with water chestnuts, green onions, chicken, shrimp, cornstarch, sugar, pepper, sesame oil, soy sauce, pepper, and oyster sauce. Lightly brush beaten egg onto won ton wrapper. Place approximately 1 rounded tablespoon of filling in center of wrapper. Bring sides of wrapper up, creating a pouch and gently squeeze until filling reaches the top of the wrapper. Gently tap the siu mai on a cutting board or other flat surface to flatten the bottom. Repeat until filling is used up. Lightly grease steamer and line bottom with lettuce leaves. Place siu mai in steamer, leaving a ½-inch space between them. Place steamer over boiling water, cover, and steam* for 12 to 15 minutes. Serve with Dipping Sauce.

Chicken Curry Crêpes

Especially good with the Mandarin Almond Salad (see page 35).

3 tablespoons butter, melted
1 cup finely chopped onion
2 teaspoons chopped parsley
3 tablespoons flour
1½ to 2 tablespoons curry powder
2 cups chicken broth
1½ cups whipping cream
2 tablespoons shredded coconut*
Salt and pepper to taste
4 cups cooked and cubed chicken breasts
¾ cup golden seedless raisins
16 crêpes (see page 117)
⅓ cup chopped peanuts

Sauté onion and parsley in butter until onion is soft but not brown. Stir in flour and curry powder and cook for one minute. Gradually stir in chicken broth and cream. When smooth, add coconut and simmer for five minutes. Add half the curry sauce to the chicken and raisins. Place 2 to 3 tablespoons of chicken mixture on each crêpe. Roll the crêpes and place seam side down in a buttered baking dish. Cover with remaining curry sauce. Crêpes may be refrigerated at this point for several hours or baked in preheated 350°F oven for 30 minutes or until sauce bubbles. Sprinkle with nuts and bake for five minutes. Garnish with Curry Condiments.

Crêpe Batter

Makes 24 crêpes

This recipe can be used for both dessert and entrée crêpes.

3 eggs
2 tablespoons sugar
1 teaspoon vanilla
Dash salt
1½ cups milk
¼ cup beer
1 cup flour
2 to 3 tablespoons melted butter

Combine ingredients in a blender and blend until smooth. Chill. Heat a 6 or 7-inch crêpe pan and coat with butter. When pan is hot, pour about 2 tablespoons batter into pan and tilt to spread evenly. Cook approximately 30 seconds or until lightly browned. Turn crêpe and cook for about 15 seconds. Re-coat pan with butter as needed.

Note: Freeze crêpes between layers of wax paper and wrap in tin foil.

Chicken with Spinach in Phyllo Cups

Serves 6

¼ cup walnut pieces or pine nuts
4 tablespoons butter melted, divided
3 sheets phyllo dough
Salt and black pepper
2 boneless chicken breasts
2 tablespoons olive oil*
3 cloves garlic, minced
1 medium onion, thinly sliced
½ cup thinly slivered oil packed sun-dried tomatoes
1½ pounds spinach, thinly sliced
8 ounces feta cheese*

Heat oven to 375°F. Spread walnuts on a small baking dish. Place in oven and bake about 5 minutes until lightly toasted, being careful not to burn. Remove from dish and set aside. Increase heat to 400°F.

Brush six large ramekins or over-sized muffin cups lightly with some of the melted butter. Set aside.

Brush one sheet of phyllo dough with melted butter. Top with second sheet. Brush with butter. Season with salt and pepper. Top with final sheet of phyllo. Cut in half lengthwise, then into thirds making six pieces. Gather up corners of each piece and carefully lay in prepared cups. Allow extra phyllo to create folds and spill over rim of cups. Gently brush inside of pastry cups with remaining butter. Bake until golden, 5 to 8 minutes. Remove from oven. Let cool in pan.

Cut chicken into thin strips and set aside. Heat oil in a skillet over medium heat. Add garlic and onion. Sauté until tender. Add chicken and sauté until cooked through. Season with salt and pepper. Stir in sun-dried tomatoes. Lay spinach on top. Cover and reduce heat. Allow steam* to cook spinach just until wilted. Stir to mix well. Remove from heat. Spoon into phyllo cups. Sprinkle with feta. Garnish with toasted nuts. Serve.

Note: Garbanzo beans (chickpeas) can be substituted for the chicken to make a vegetarian version.

Chicken Assaggio   *Serves 2*

6 tablespoons extra virgin olive oil*
½ pound boneless chicken, skinned and cut into bite-sized
  pieces
Salt and freshly ground pepper to taste
2 cloves garlic, chopped
½ teaspoon basil
6 medium pepperoncini,* cut into strips
½ cup green bell pepper, roasted and cut into strips
½ cup mushrooms, sliced
¼ cup black olives, sliced
1 teaspoon capers*
¼ cup dry white wine
¼ cup butter
8 ounces linguine or spaghettini, cooked
Garnish: fresh chopped parsley and fresh chopped basil

Heat olive oil in a large skillet. Add chicken and stir-fry for
3 to 5 minutes. Add salt, pepper, garlic, and basil. Cook for
another 2 minutes. Add pepperoncini, sweet roasted pepper,
mushrooms, black olives, and capers. Cook, stirring until the
vegetables are barely tender. Reduce heat to low and stir in wine
and butter. Serve over pasta. Garnish with fresh parsley and
basil.

To roast bell pepper, halve lengthwise and remove the seeds.
Place pieces lengthwise on a broiler pan. Broil peppers until
brown blisters appear on the skin. Peel and slice into strips.

Maui Lavender
Spiced Cornish Hens

Serves 6

6 Cornish game hens or one large roasting chicken
1 cup dry white wine
¼ cup Cognac or brandy
1 teaspoon Worcestershire sauce
1 teaspoon hot pepper sauce,* such as Tabasco
2 tablespoons fresh thyme
1 tablespoon dried lavender flowers
1 tablespoon celery salt
1 teaspoon white pepper
3 cloves garlic, minced
Sprigs of fresh thyme and lavender

Rinse and pat dry game hens. Pack in a single layer in a non-reactive deep pan or plastic container. Combine wine, Cognac, Worcestershire, and hot sauce. Pour over hens. Cover and refrigerate at least 6 hours or overnight, turning or basting occasionally.

Heat oven to 425°F. In a spice mill, food processor, or small bowl, combine thyme, lavender, celery salt, pepper, and garlic. Whirl or mash together to blend. Drain hens, discarding marinade. Rub each hen with some of the herb mixture. Arrange in roasting pan. Place in center of oven and bake 1½ hours, basting occasionally (if using large roasting chicken, bake about 2 hours), until juices run clear. Remove from oven, let stand 5 to 10 minutes before serving. Garnish with fresh thyme and lavender.

Note: Lavender is grown in the uplands of Maui along the slopes of Haleakalā. Edible lavender flower buds can be ordered from Maui but are also available at natural food stores.

Baked Kūmū

2 pounds whole kūmū,* red snapper or sea bass
Salt and pepper
1 tablespoon fresh lemon juice
Dried fennel leaves (optional)
½ cup butter
½ to 1 cup thinly sliced onion
3 tablespoons butter
2 medium potatoes, peeled and thinly sliced
2 medium tomatoes, quartered
½ cup white wine
3 tablespoons Pernod
Garnish: chopped parsley and 1 lemon, quartered

Preheat oven to 375°F. Season fish inside and out with salt, pepper, and lemon juice. Place fennel leaves inside fish. Melt butter and brown fish on both sides. Place fish and remaining butter in baking dish and bake for 10 minutes. Sauté onion in 3 tablespoons butter and place around the fish, baking an additional 10 minutes. Parboil the potatoes in salted water. Add potatoes to the fish and bake for an additional 20 minutes. Add tomatoes and pour the wine over the fish. Sprinkle with Pernod. Bake for 8 minutes. Place fish on a serving platter. Arrange vegetables around the fish. Pour juices from the baking dish over the fish and garnish.

Maile Restaurant
Kahala Hilton
Honolulu, Hawai'i

Kona Inn Onaga

Serves 1 to 2

Can be prepared in advance and refrigerated until ready to bake.

8 ounces onaga,* deboned
Flour
2 tablespoons butter
3 ounces green chili salsa
2 ounces Monterey Jack cheese, shredded
1 ounce Cheddar cheese, shredded
Salt and pepper
Garnish: chopped parsley

Preheat oven to 350°F. Lightly flour fish and sauté in butter for approximately one minute on each side to seal in juices. Put fish in casserole and top with salsa. Sprinkle Cheddar cheese on center of fish and Monterey Jack on each end. Bake for 10 to 12 minutes. Garnish with chopped parsley.

Kona Inn Restaurant
Kailua Kona, Hawai'i

Fillet of Sole with Lychee *Serves 4 to 6*

Fish Poaching Liquid
1½ to 2 cups chicken or fish stock
½ to ¾ cup white wine
2 shallots, minced
3 green onion tops, chopped
Dash white pepper

Bring ingredients to a boil in a flat sauté pan or metal gratin pan.

Fish
8 sole fillets or ʻōpakapaka*
16 seedless grapes
16 lychee,* canned or fresh (pitted and peeled)
3 tablespoons butter

Break line on fillets by tapping lightly with knife to facilitate rolling. Cut down spine, dividing in two. Place rough side up and salt lightly. Stuff lychee with seedless grapes and roll one in each strip of sole. Secure with toothpicks. Turn heat off poaching liquid and place rolls in the liquid. Add 2 tablespoons butter and cover with 10 x 14-inch sheet of brown paper bag (not recycled) which has been heavily buttered with 1 tablespoon butter. Place buttered side over fish and bake on lowest rack in oven for 7 to 10 minutes at 475°F. Remove from oven and place in ovenproof serving dish. Cover and set aside.

Velouté Sauce
Reduced poaching liquid
1½ cups half-and-half
1 tablespoon butter
1 tablespoon flour
Freshly grated nutmeg
Dash white pepper
Salt to taste
¼ to ⅓ cup grated Swiss cheese
Juice of ½ lemon
Garnish: minced parsley

Strain poaching liquid into a saucepan and boil down to half (6 to 7 minutes). Heat half-and-half to near boil. Make a roux in a 1-quart saucepan by melting butter and stirring in flour. Cook at medium heat for 1 minute. Do not brown. Remove roux from heat and stir in hot half-and-half and mix vigorously with a wire whisk. Add half of the reduced poaching liquid, nutmeg, white pepper, and salt. Bring to a slow boil and add Swiss cheese, stirring constantly with a whisk. Add lemon juice. Pour the sauce evenly over the poached sole rolls and place under the broiler for 2 to 3 minutes or until the sauce is bubbling. Allow to stay until it begins to turn a slightly golden color in places. Garnish and serve.

Nino J. Martin
The International Chef © Hawaii Public Television
Honolulu, Hawai'i

'Ōpakapaka with Shrimp and Almonds

Serves 1

7 ounce 'ōpakapaka* fillet
4 ounces clarified butter, melted
2 ounces clam juice
Juice of ½ lemon
½ teaspoon seasoning salt

Shrimp and Almond Sauce
2 to 3 shrimp
¼ cup almonds, sliced or slivered
2 to 3 tablespoons butter
Dash seasoning salt
½ ounce white wine
Garnish: chopped parsley

Preheat oven to 375°F. Place fish and remaining ingredients in an ovenproof baking dish and bake for 10 minutes. In a separate skillet, sauté shrimp and almonds in butter. Add salt and wine. Place fish on the plate. Top with shrimp and almonds. Lace the sauce over the fish and garnish with chopped parsley.

Alfred "Almar" Arcano
Executive Chef
Hy's Steak House
Honolulu, Hawai'i

Plaza Club Mahimahi

Serves 4

½ cup mayonnaise
2 tablespoons lemon juice
2 ounces crabmeat
¼ cup finely diced celery
¾ pound dash avocado, finely diced
Dash Worcestershire sauce
Salt and pepper to taste
4 (5-ounce) mahimahi* fillets

Preheat oven to 350°F. Combine mayonnaise, lemon juice, crabmeat, celery, and avocado. Season with Worcestershire, salt, and pepper. Place fillets in a lightly buttered baking pan and spread evenly with avocado mixture. Do not let the thickness of the mixture exceed ½ inch. Bake for 10 to 15 minutes.

Russell Siu
Plaza Club
Honolulu, Hawai'i

Broiled Tuna Steaks

¾ cup olive oil*
Salt and freshly ground pepper to taste
1 bay leaf
½ onion, chopped
2 tuna steaks (2 to 2½ pounds)
2 cloves garlic, chopped
2 tablespoons parsley, chopped
2 tablespoons capers,* chopped

Combine ½ cup olive oil, salt, pepper, bay leaf, and onion. Marinate tuna in seasoned oil for 1 hour. Preheat the broiler. Remove the tuna from the marinade and place on a broiling rack that has been preheated for 10 minutes. Broil the fish 4 inches from heat, brushing the steaks occasionally with marinade. Cook evenly on both sides for about 10 minutes or until flesh is opaque. Combine remaining ¼ cup olive oil, garlic, parsley, and capers and pour over top of fish. Serve immediately.

Dijon Tomato Fish Pouches

Serves 8

A different way to barbecue fish that leaves your grill clean!

8 (6-ounce) fresh fish fillets, 'ōpakapaka* or onaga*
Salt and freshly ground pepper to taste
3 medium shallots, minced
3 medium cloves garlic, minced
¾ cup vegetable oil
¼ cup Dijon mustard*
2 tablespoons fresh lemon juice
1 tablespoon dried basil
1 pound fresh plum tomatoes,* thinly sliced
2 tablespoons fresh chives, snipped
Garnish: fresh parsley

Prepare barbecue. Cut pieces of foil large enough to wrap each serving of fish. Sprinkle fish with salt and pepper and set on foil. Combine shallots, garlic, oil, mustard, lemon juice, and basil and mix well. Spread over fish. Cover each piece of fish with tomato slices and sprinkle with salt, pepper, and chives. Wrap tightly leaving space above fish for steam to collect. Place on grill and cook until fish is firm to the touch and no longer translucent, about 10 to 12 minutes. Remove foil, transfer to serving platter and garnish with parsley.

Seared and Smoked 'Ahi with Pistachio Pesto, Ogo Wasabi Sauce and Radish Salsa

Serves 4

The condiments can be made ahead for this exotic entrée.

1 (12-ounce) piece sashimi grade 'ahi,* cut into strips
6 ounces Pistachio Pesto
6 ounces Ogo Wasabi Sauce
1½ cups Radish Salsa
1 ounce olive oil*
Garnish: 4 small bunches ogo* and ½ cup finely chopped
    Chinese parsley*

Brush 'ahi strips with pistachio pesto. Sear 'ahi in olive oil on all sides, keeping the fish raw in the center. Lightly smoke 'ahi for approximately 10 to 15 minutes. Cut into slices ¼-inch thick and lay across serving platter. Ladle wasabi sauce over one half of the fish slices and pesto over the other half. Spoon salsa in the middle of the platter. Garnish with ogo bunches and chopped Chinese parsley.

Pistachio Pesto
¼ cup pistachio nuts, lightly toasted in the oven
3 cloves garlic, sautéed until light brown
½ cup extra virgin olive oil*
½ cup Parmesan cheese,* grated
¼ teaspoon freshly ground black pepper
1 cup fresh basil, chopped
Salt to taste

Purée all ingredients in a food processor.

Ogo Wasabi Sauce

½ teaspoon wasabi* paste
¼ teaspoon dry mustard paste
1 teaspoon Dijon mustard*
3 tablespoon soy sauce*
4 tablespoons plain yogurt
2 tablespoons chopped dill
2 tablespoons ogo,* finely chopped
1 teaspoon 'inomona,* finely chopped (optional)

Mix all ingredients together

Radish Salsa

3 tablespoons red radish
2 tablespoons daikon*
3 tablespoons lychee*
2 tablespoons jicama*
2 tablespoons Maui onion*
2 tablespoons cucumber
1 ounce olive oil*
½ teaspoon sesame oil*
1 tablespoon Chinese parsley*
1 teaspoon opal basil*
¾ ounce lime juice
1 ounce rice wine*
¼ teaspoon chili pepper
Salt to taste

Dice radish, daikon, lychee, jicama, onion, and cucumber into ⅛-inch pieces and combine in a stainless steel bowl. Add olive oil, sesame oil, Chinese parsley, opal basil, lime juice, rice wine, chili pepper, and salt and mix well. Adjust seasoning and chill.

'Ahi Wraps

Sauce
½ cup mayonnaise
1 teaspoon prepared wasabi*

Slaw
2 ounces fresh snow pea pods, trimmed
1 small head Napa cabbage, trimmed, washed, and shredded
1 carrot, peeled and shredded
2 scallions, finely sliced
3 tablespoons coarsely chopped cilantro*
3 tablespoons slivered almonds
1-inch piece fresh ginger* root, grated
1 clove garlic minced
1 tablespoon olive oil*
1 teaspoon sesame oil*
1 teaspoon granulated sugar
1 tablespoon rice vinegar*
2 tablespoons fresh lime juice
Salt and black pepper

Wraps
8 large whole wheat tortillas
12 ounces fresh tuna steak
1 teaspoon olive oil*
1 to 2 ounces enoki mushrooms, washed and patted dry

In a small bowl, combine mayonnaise and wasabi, mixing well. Cover and refrigerate. Place pea pods in a small saucepan with a little water. Bring to a boil over high heat and steam* 30 seconds until bright green. Drain and rinse under cold water. Remove to cutting board and slice lengthwise into thin strips. Set aside. Place cabbage in large mixing bowl. Add carrot, scallions, cilantro, and almonds and set aside.

In a small bowl combine ginger, garlic, olive oil, sesame oil, sugar, vinegar, and lime juice. Whisk together until well-blended. Pour over vegetables. Toss to coat. Season with salt and pepper to taste. Spread 1 tablespoon of wasabi mayonnaise evenly over each tortilla. Do not stack but set each aside separately.

Heat a skillet over medium-high heat. Rub tuna steak with olive oil and place in hot skillet. Sear tuna, cooking each side about 2 minutes. Remove from pan. Let rest a few minutes before slicing thinly into 16 pieces. Using tongs and dividing equally, pick up vegetable slaw, shake gently to rid of excess dressing, and arrange down center of each tortilla. Top with snow pea pods, saving a few for garnish.

Arrange tuna slices on top of vegetable slaw. Top with enoki mushrooms, saving a few for garnish. Fold in sides of tortilla and roll to create a wrapped sandwich. Place seam side down on serving platter. Garnish with reserved pea pods and mushrooms. Serve.

Coconut Crusted Snapper   *Serves 4*

2 tablespoons oil
1 cup flour
1 egg
⅓ cup milk
3 cups shredded coconut*
4 red snapper fillets
4 teaspoons fresh lime juice
4 fresh Thai chilies, minced
Salt

Heat oil in a frying pan over medium heat. Place flour in a shallow dish. Beat egg with milk in a medium bowl. Place coconut in a shallow dish. Dust each fish fillet in flour, dip in egg-milk mixture letting excess drip off, and place in coconut, pressing lightly to adhere. Lay coated fish in hot pan. Sauté 4 minutes, then turn. Continue to sauté 4 to 6 minutes, until fish flakes easily with a fork. Remove to serving platter. Sprinkle with lime juice, chilies, and salt. Serve.

Note: Thai chilies are available in specialty produce sections or at Asian markets.

The Willows
Shrimp Curry

Serves 6

Curry Sauce
6 tablespoons clarified butter
3 cloves garlic, minced
¼ cup chopped fresh ginger*
2 cups finely chopped onions
3 teaspoons salt
3 teaspoons sugar
3 tablespoons curry powder
9 tablespoons flour
2 quarts coconut milk*

Sauté garlic, ginger, and onion in clarified butter. Add salt, sugar, curry powder, and flour. Mix thoroughly. Add coconut milk a little at a time, stirring to a smooth thickness and cook for 20 minutes until sauce begins to boil. Allow to stand several hours. Strain before using.

2 pounds shrimp (preferably 21 to 25 count per pound)
6 ounces white wine or dry vermouth
3 tablespoons peanut oil*
Salt and pepper to taste
6 tablespoons curry powder

Peel shrimp. Cut lengthwise in half. Devein and wash. Marinate shrimp in white wine or dry vermouth and peanut oil. Add pinch of salt and pepper. Let stand 15 minutes. Pan fry curry powder in saucepan. Add marinated shrimp. When shrimp turns pink, pour in curry sauce.

Note: Chicken is prepared in same manner.

The Willows
Honolulu, Hawai'i

'Aiea Paella

1 tablespoon paprika
2 teaspoons dried oregano
1 teaspoon Hawaiian sea salt
1 teaspoon black pepper
2 pounds boneless chicken thighs
3 cups medium-grained rice
5 to 6 cups water
15 ounces canned diced tomatoes
¼ cup chopped parsley
1 pound Portuguese sausage,* thickly sliced
2 'Ewa sweet onions, diced
6 garlic cloves, crushed
1 pound jumbo shrimp, peeled and deveined
1 pound sea scallops
1 cup frozen green peas, thawed
Lemon wedges

Mix together paprika, oregano, salt, and pepper in a small bowl. Cut chicken into 1-inch pieces. Place chicken in a glass bowl, sprinkle with spices, and rub in. If time permits, cover, and marinate for 1 hour in refrigerator.

In a large pot, combine rice and water. Bring to a boil over high heat, reduce heat to low, cover, and cook 20 minutes until tender. Stir in tomatoes and parsley. Set aside.

Heat a large skillet over medium heat. Add sausage and cook until browned. Drain fat. Remove to a large bowl and set aside. Add chicken and cook until browned. Remove and set aside with sausage. Add onions and garlic. Sauté 5 to 8 minutes until soft. Stir shrimp and scallops into onions. Cook 3 minutes stirring and tossing until opaque. Add peas and cook 1 minute. Remove from heat.

Gently stir sausage and chicken into rice. Spoon shrimp and scallops over rice and gently fold in with a few swift strokes. Garnish with lemon and serve.

Note: True paella is made in one large paella pan on the stove with ingredients slowly added as it cooks.

Kahuku Prawns   *Serves 4*

Prawns are grown commercially on O'ahu's North shore.

3 tablespoons olive oil*
12 prawns, shelled (except tail), split and cleaned
¼ cup butter
1 small clove garlic, crushed
¼ teaspoon salt
¼ teaspoon freshly ground pepper
¼ cup dry vermouth
3 tablespoons lemon juice

Sauté prawns in olive oil on high heat until golden brown. Reduce heat and add butter, garlic, salt, and pepper. Stir to blend. Transfer cooked prawns to a heated platter. To pan juices, add dry vermouth and lemon juice. Cook for one minute, stirring constantly and pour over prawns.

Buzzy's Vermouth Scallops   *Serves 4*

By itself or served over rice, this dish is elegant.

1 to 1½ pounds scallops
½ cup dry vermouth
¼ cup butter
½ teaspoon salt
⅛ teaspoon ground pepper
¼ teaspoon paprika
4 to 5 cloves garlic, minced
1 tablespoon minced parsley
3 tablespoons lemon juice

Marinate scallops in vermouth for several hours in the refrigerator. Heat 2 tablespoons butter in a large skillet. Add salt, pepper, paprika, and garlic. Add scallops and cook quickly over high heat, stirring occasionally until golden brown (5 to 10 minutes). Transfer to a heated platter. To pan juices, add parsley, lemon juice, and remaining butter. Heat and pour over scallops.

Sunset Sea Scallops

2 tablespoons frozen orange juice concentrate, thawed
1 teaspoon Dijon mustard*
Freshly ground black pepper
2 tablespoons extra-virgin olive oil*
2 tablespoons fresh basil, chopped
Salt to taste
2 tablespoons olive oil*
1½ pounds fresh scallops
1½ pounds fresh spinach, washed, trimmed and torn in bite-size pieces
2 teaspoons orange peel, finely grated

In a small bowl, whisk together orange juice, mustard, and pepper. Slowly stir in olive oil. Add 1 tablespoon basil and season with salt. Set aside. Heat olive oil in a large skillet. Over medium heat, cook half of the scallops at a time for 4 to 5 minutes or until opaque and lightly browned. While scallops are cooking, steam* the spinach in the moisture that clings to the leaves until tender, about 3 minutes. When scallops are done, drain the spinach and arrange on a large serving platter. Center the scallops on the spinach and pour orange dressing on top. Garnish with remaining basil and orange zest and serve immediately.

Vegetables

Asparagus Sesame

2 pounds fresh asparagus
2 tablespoons vegetable oil
1 tablespoon sesame oil*
1 tablespoon soy sauce*
2 teaspoons brown sugar
Garnish: toasted sesame seeds*

Trim ends from asparagus. Place spears in a bowl for steaming. Mix oils, soy sauce, and sugar. Pour over asparagus. Steam* covered for 15 minutes. Garnish.

Note: Asparagus may be served in spears or cut in 2-inch diagonal pieces.

Italian Marinated Vegetables

Serves 8

1(8-ounce) can button mushrooms
1 green pepper, cut into ½-inch strips
1 carrot, chopped
2 cups cauliflower flowerets
1 (14-ounce) can artichoke hearts, drained
12 green onions, chopped
½ cup pimiento stuffed olives
1½ cups red wine vinegar*
1 teaspoon sugar
1½ teaspoons salt
½ teaspoon pepper
2 teaspoons oregano
2 teaspoons crushed red pepper flakes
2 tablespoons Dijon mustard*
½ cup olive oil*
12 ounces cherry tomatoes, cut in half
2 tablespoons minced parsley

Combine mushrooms, green pepper, carrot, cauliflower, artichokes, onions, and olives. Heat vinegar and stir in sugar and seasonings. Cool slightly, then add oil. Pour over vegetables and mix. Cover and refrigerate for 24 hours, stirring periodically. Add tomatoes and parsley when ready to serve.

Sherried Kula Onions

¼ cup butter
5 medium Kula or Maui onions,* thinly sliced or
    3 large onions, thinly sliced
½ teaspoon sugar
½ teaspoon salt
½ teaspoon freshly ground pepper
½ cup sherry
¼ cup fresh Parmesan cheese,* grated
Dash nutmeg

Melt butter in a medium skillet over medium heat. Add onions, sugar, salt, and pepper. Cook over low heat until soft, about 5 to 8 minutes. Increase heat, add sherry, and cook for 2 to 3 minutes. Sprinkle with Parmesan cheese and nutmeg and serve.

Kabocha Pumpkin with Caramelized Onions

Serves 6

2 pounds Kabocha pumpkin
½ cup water
½ cup golden raisins
½ cup warm water
¼ cup olive oil*
2 large Maui onions* thinly sliced
¼ cup sliced almonds
¼ cup granulated sugar
1 teaspoon ground cinnamon
Salt and black pepper
Sliced almonds

Heat oven to 375°F. Slice pumpkin into 1-inch wedges and peel.

Place in an ovenproof baking dish. Add ½ cup water and cover tightly. Bake until tender about 45 to 50 minutes. Place raisins in small bowl. Cover with warm water and let plump. In a large skillet over medium-low, heat oil and cook onions, stirring occasionally, 20 to 25 minutes until caramelized. Drain raisins and add to skillet with almonds, sugar, and cinnamon. Cook, stirring, for 5 more minutes. Drain off any excess water from cooked pumpkin. Season with salt and pepper. Spread onion mixture evenly over pumpkin. Sprinkle with additional almonds and serve.

Note: Sugar pumpkins or acorn squash may be substituted for Kabocha.

Stir-Fried Ung Choi with Miso

Serves 6

2 pounds fresh ung choi
2 tablespoons soy sauce*
1 tablespoon miso*
2 teaspoons rice vinegar*
2 tablespoons sliced almonds
1 tablespoon peanut oil*
1 teaspoon sesame oil*
1 teaspoon grated fresh ginger* root

Wash ung choi, trim ends, and cut into 2-inch pieces. Set aside. Combine soy sauce, miso, and vinegar until smooth. Set aside. Heat a wok* over high heat. Add almonds and stir-fry quickly until fragrant and toasted, about 45 seconds. Remove almonds and set aside.

Add peanut and sesame oils to wok and heat. Add ung choi and ginger and stir-fry until greens are tender, 2 to 3 minutes. Sprinkle with soy sauce mixture and heat through allowing sauce to reduce and thicken. Place in a serving bowl. Sprinkle with toasted sliced almonds and serve.

Ali'i Artichoke Casserole

Serves 8

3 (10-ounce) packages frozen chopped spinach
2 (14-ounce) cans artichoke hearts, drained and cut in half
8 ounces cream cheese
½ cup butter
2 tablespoons Worcestershire sauce
1 teaspoon salt
½ teaspoon garlic powder
½ teaspoon pepper
⅛ teaspoon cayenne
⅛ teaspoon Tabasco
1 tablespoon lemon juice
½ cup Italian-seasoned bread crumbs

Preheat oven to 350°F. Cook spinach and drain well. Melt the butter and cream cheese. Add seasonings, lemon juice, and spinach, mixing after each addition. In a greased 2-quart casserole place a layer of artichoke hearts, then a layer of spinach mixture and repeat. Top with bread crumbs. Bake for 30 minutes.

Sweet Potato Casserole   *Serves 6 to 8*

The coconut adds a tropical twist to an old favorite.

4 cups sweet potatoes, cooked and mashed or 2 (24-ounce)
    cans sweet potatoes or yams, drained
2 tablespoons sugar
⅓ cup butter
½ cup milk
2 eggs, beaten
⅓ cup flaked coconut*
⅓ cup pecans, chopped
⅓ cup brown sugar
2 tablespoons butter, melted

Preheat oven to 325°F. Beat sweet potatoes, sugar, butter, milk, and eggs until light and fluffy. Pour into a 2-quart casserole. Mix coconut, pecans, brown sugar, and melted butter and sprinkle on top of the sweet potatoes. Bake at 325°F for 1 hour or until potatoes are heated through and top is crunchy.

Thai Eggplant with Basil
Serves 4

½ cup coconut milk*
2 tablespoons oil
16 small green Thai eggplant, trimmed and quartered
2 cloves garlic, minced
1 to 2 teaspoons green curry paste, homemade or prepared
2 tablespoons fish sauce*
1 teaspoon granulated sugar
½ cup broth or water
2 kaffir lime leaves
20 basil leaves

Green Curry Paste
2 long green chilies, minced
10 small green chilies, minced
1 tablespoon chopped lemongrass
3 shallots, minced
2 tablespoons minced garlic
1-inch piece galangal or fresh ginger* root, minced
1 tablespoon minced cilantro*
1 teaspoon ground coriander seed
½ teaspoon ground cumin
½ teaspoon ground white pepper
1 teaspoon chopped kaffir lime leaves
2 teaspoons shrimp paste
1 teaspoon salt

In a small saucepan, gently warm coconut milk over medium-low heat, do not allow to boil. Set aside.

In a frying pan or wok*, heat oil over medium-high heat until it starts smoking. Add eggplant and garlic. Fry until golden. Add curry paste and stir-fry a few seconds. Add warmed coconut milk and stir until thickened. Add fish sauce, sugar, and broth. Reduce heat and simmer 3 to 4 minutes, stirring occasionally.

Add lime leaves and basil, stir and cook 1 minute. Place into serving dish. Serve hot.

Green Curry Paste: Using a mortar and pestle or spice grinder, blend all ingredients together to form a smooth paste. Keep refrigerated.

Note: Galangal is a Thai ginger root.

Vegetable Curry

Serve on a bed of hot, fluffy rice

¼ cup vegetable oil
½ cup onion, chopped
3 tablespoons unsweetened coconut,* chopped
4 teaspoons curry powder
2 to 3 cloves garlic, minced
2 pounds assorted raw vegetables (potatoes, cauliflower, broccoli, carrots, zucchini, etc.), cut into bite-size pieces
3 cups tomatoes, peeled and diced
2 cups water
2 teaspoons salt
4 teaspoons sugar
Dash thyme

Heat oil in large skillet with cover. Add onion, coconut, curry powder, and garlic. Cook, stirring occasionally, until onion is tender. Add vegetables, tomato, water, salt, sugar, and thyme. Cover tightly and cook over low heat until vegetables are tender approximately 45 minutes.

Armenian Vegetable Stew   *Serves 4*

A full-bodied vegetable stew that may be served hot or cold.

1 large onion, chopped
5 tablespoons olive oil,* divided
4 stalks celery, cut into 1-inch pieces
2 cups green beans, cut into 2-inch pieces
1 (28-ounce) can whole tomatoes, including juice, coarsely
    chopped or 4 cups freshly chopped tomatoes plus 1 cup
    tomato juice
3 bay leaves
3 large cloves garlic, pressed
2 tablespoons fresh basil, finely chopped or 2 teaspoons dried
    basil
½ teaspoon ground thyme
1 medium round eggplant or 3 small long eggplants, cut into
    ¾-inch pieces
Salt and freshly ground pepper
1½ tablespoons lemon juice
Garnish: lemon slices

In a large pot, sauté onions in 3 tablespoons of olive oil over medium heat until onions are translucent. Add celery, stir, cover, and cook for 5 minutes. Add green beans, tomatoes, bay leaves, garlic, basil, and thyme; stir, cover, and cook for 7 minutes. Place eggplant on top of the vegetables. Sprinkle with salt and pepper and drizzle with 2 tablespoons of olive oil. Cover and simmer for 20 minutes. Stir occasionally but do not let the eggplant touch the bottom of the pan and burn. After eggplant has released its juices, stir it in and continue simmering until eggplant and vegetables are tender. Stir in lemon juice. Garnish with lemon slices.

Ratatouille

This tastes great served over angel hair pasta.

1½ pounds zucchini, cut into 2-inch lengths
1¼ pounds eggplant, cubed
2 teaspoons salt
2 large onions, diced
1 green bell pepper, seeded and diced
1 cup fresh Chinese parsley,* minced
2 large cloves garlic, minced
2 medium tomatoes, coarsely chopped
¼ cup olive oil*
1 teaspoon ground coriander
1 teaspoon crushed thyme
1½ teaspoons dried basil
3 rounded tablespoons tomato paste
¼ cup tomato sauce
Salt and pepper to taste
1 to 1½ teaspoons sugar
Garnish: chopped Chinese parsley*

Preheat oven to 350°F. Place zucchini and eggplant in colander. Sprinkle with 2 teaspoons salt and drain for 30 minutes. Pat vegetables dry with paper towels. In a large pot, sauté onion and pepper in olive oil for 3 minutes. Add eggplant and zucchini. Cover and let steam* on medium heat for 10 minutes. Stir in Chinese parsley garlic, tomatoes, coriander, thyme, basil, tomato paste, and tomato sauce. Simmer 10 minutes, uncovered. Add salt, pepper, and sugar to taste.

Transfer to an ovenproof casserole, cover, and bake until soft about 40 minutes. Garnish with Chinese parsley. Serve at room temperature or cold.

Vegetarian Chili with Pink Onion Relish

Serves 6 to 8

1 small green bell pepper, chopped
1 small red bell pepper, chopped
⅓ cup celery, chopped
2 large onions, chopped
3 tablespoons vegetable oil
1 tablespoon mustard seed
2 tablespoons chili powder
1 teaspoon cumin seed
1 teaspoon unsweetened cocoa
1 teaspoon oregano
¼ teaspoon cinnamon
1 (14½-ounce) can whole tomatoes, including juice,
     broken into large chunks
3 (8¾-ounce) cans kidney beans, with juice
1 (6-ounce) can tomato paste
1 cup water
Salt and pepper to taste
Pink Onion Relish (see page 186)
Garnish: grated cheddar cheese, sliced green peppers,
     chopped cucumbers, and chopped tomatoes

Sauté peppers, celery, and onions in oil in a medium-sized saucepan until onions are golden brown and peppers are barely tender. Add mustard seed and cook for 1 minute, stirring constantly. Add chili powder, cumin seed, oregano, cinnamon, tomatoes, kidney beans, tomato paste, water, salt and pepper. Simmer for 40 minutes or until thickened, stirring occasionally Garnish and serve.

Eggs, Rice, and Pasta

Benedict Local Style

Serves 2 to 4

Cakes
1 cup sushi rice
1¼ cups water
¼ teaspoon salt

Hollandaise Sauce
2 egg yolks
4 tablespoons cream
2 tablespoons butter
Juice of ½ lemon
Pinch salt
Pinch sugar
Chicken broth
1 tablespoon white vinegar

Topping
3 tablespoons unsalted butter divided
8 slices Canadian bacon
4 eggs
⅛ teaspoon salt
⅛ teaspoon black pepper
1 scallion, trimmed and thinly sliced

Rinse rice in a large fine-mesh sieve under cold running water. Drain well. Combine rice, water, and salt in a 2-quart heavy saucepan and bring to a boil over high heat. Reduce heat to low and cook, covered, 15 minutes. Remove from heat and let stand, covered, 10 minutes.

Stir rice from bottom to top. Lightly grease a metal 1-cup measure. Firmly pack enough rice in measure using rubber spatula to fill halfway. If spatula becomes sticky, dip in water. Invert onto a buttered plate, tapping to unmold rice.

Repeat with remaining rice, greasing mold each time, to make four cakes. Chill, uncovered, at least 15 minutes.

Combine egg yolks, cream, butter, lemon juice, salt, and sugar in the top of a double boiler, over boiling water. Stir until thick, approximately 3 minutes. Set aside, leaving pot over hot water. Thin, if needed, with a little chicken broth. Stir in the vinegar. Do not reheat or cover the pot.

Melt 1 tablespoon butter in a large nonstick skillet over medium-low heat. Add rice cakes and cook, until pale golden, about 8 to 10 minutes. Turn cakes, add ½ tablespoon butter and cook until other side is golden, about 5 minutes. Transfer to plates.

Increase heat to medium-high and melt ½ tablespoon butter in skillet. Add Canadian bacon and cook, turning once, about 1 minute per side until browned. Place 2 slices bacon on each rice cake.

Melt remaining tablespoon butter. Crack eggs one by one into skillet. Sprinkle with salt and pepper and fry until whites are cooked and yolks begin to set, 2 to 4 minutes. Turn and cook other side. Place 1 egg on each stack and top with some Hollandaise sauce. Sprinkle with scallion and serve.

Note: Sushi rice cooks up slightly moist and sticky, forming a cake easily. Chilling the cakes before browning helps to hold their shape. Rice cakes can be shaped one day ahead. Allow to cool 15 minutes before covering and refrigerating. Allow 2 to 5 minutes longer to heat.

Artichoke Quiche

Serves 6

1 (9-inch) pie shell
2 tablespoons butter
½ cup chopped green onion
2 eggs
1 tablespoon flour
⅔ cup half-and-half
¼ teaspoon garlic salt
1 (14-ounce) can artichoke hearts, drained and coarsely
    chopped
1 cup grated Hot Pepper cheese
1 cup grated Cheddar cheese

Preheat oven to 400°F. Pierce bottom of pie shell and bake for 12 minutes. Reduce oven to 350°F. In a small skillet sauté the onion in butter. In a large bowl, beat the eggs, flour, and cream together. Stir in the garlic salt, artichokes, Hot Pepper cheese, Cheddar cheese, and the onion-butter mixture. Stir until well-blended. Pour into the pastry shell and bake for 45 minutes or until firm in the center.

Seafood Quiche

Makes 2 quiches

2 (9-inch) deep dish pie shells
6 ounces frozen king crabmeat, thawed and drained
1½ cups shrimp, cooked, shelled, deveined and chopped
1 pound Swiss cheese, grated
½ to 1 cup finely chopped celery
½ cup finely chopped green onion
1 cup mayonnaise
2 tablespoons flour
½ to 1 cup dry white wine
4 eggs, slightly beaten

Preheat oven to 350°F. Combine crabmeat, shrimp, cheese, celery, and green onion. Divide seafood mixture equally between pie shells. Combine mayonnaise, flour, white wine, and eggs. Divide mayonnaise mixture equally between pie shells, pouring evenly over seafood. Bake 40 to 45 minutes or until firm in center.

Note: If quiches are to be frozen, do not bake before freezing.

Spinach Pie

Serves 6 to 8

This is a delight to the eye and the palate.

1 (9-inch) deep dish pie shell, baked
1 (10-ounce) package frozen spinach
3 tablespoons butter
1 small onion, minced
1 to 2 cloves garlic, minced
2 cups finely chopped mushrooms
4 eggs
8 ounces cream cheese, softened
8 ounces Kasseri cheese, grated
8 ounces feta cheese*, crumbled
1 cup grated Swiss cheese
¼ to ⅓ cup grated Parmesan cheese*

Preheat oven to 350°F. Thaw and drain spinach. Sauté onion and garlic in butter. Add mushrooms and cook for 3 to 5 minutes. Drain juices and set aside. Combine eggs and cream cheese. In bottom of pie shell, layer ⅓ of the Kasseri, all of the garlic, onion, and mushroom mixture, ½ of the egg and cream cheese mix, balance of Kasseri, all of the spinach (squeezing out all excess water), crumbled feta cheese, balance of egg mixture, all of the Swiss cheese, and all of the Parmesan cheese. Bake for 45 minutes.

Furikake Pan Sushi

Serves 10 to 12

A simple Oriental rice treat that is full of flavor as well as color.

½ cup rice vinegar*
½ cup sugar
1 teaspoon salt
8 cups hot cooked white rice

Combine vinegar, sugar, and salt, stirring until sugar is dissolved. Pour over rice and mix until well-absorbed. Press into a 9 x 13-inch pan. Precut into 3 x 3-inch servings.

Topping
3 egg omelet, julienned
1 (.85-ounce) bottle furikake*
¼ cup pickled ginger slivers*
½ cup fish cake* strips
6 to 8 string beans, blanched and julienned
½ cup julienned ham, chicken, or turkey
2 tablespoons green hana ebi*
2 tablespoons red hana ebi*

Sprinkle ingredients evenly over rice. Cover pan with foil until ready to serve. Do not refrigerate as rice will dry out.

Paniolo Spanish Rice

Serves 8 to 10

Good served with cole slaw.

¼ cup water
1 cup onion, chopped
¾ cup green bell pepper, chopped
1 cup uncooked rice
3½ cups stewed tomatoes, drained and coarsely chopped
1 teaspoon salt
½ teaspoon freshly ground pepper
1 small bay leaf
1 teaspoon cumin
1 (4-ounce) can mild chili peppers, diced
½ cup Cheddar cheese, shredded

Preheat oven to 350°F. Combine all ingredients except cheese and pour into a 2-quart casserole. Cover and bake for 1 hour and 15 minutes, stirring occasionally. During the last ten minutes of baking time, remove cover and sprinkle with cheese.

Sweet Curry Pilaf

Serves 6 to 8

4 tablespoons vegetable oil
½ teaspoon curry powder
½ teaspoon tumeric
2 cups long grain rice
4 cups chicken broth
1½ tablespoons soy sauce*
½ cup golden raisins

In saucepan, combine oil, curry, turmeric, and rice. Cook over low heat for 5 minutes, stirring occasionally. Add chicken broth, soy sauce, and raisins and heat to boiling. Stir, cover, and simmer over low heat until liquid is absorbed, about 15 to 20 minutes.

Barley Mushroom Pilaf

Serves 4

2 tablespoons butter
1 medium onion, thinly sliced
2 cloves garlic minced
1 teaspoon fresh thyme
¼ teaspoon black pepper
8 ounces mushrooms thinly sliced
¼ teaspoon sea salt
2½ cups chicken broth
¾ cup pearl barley
Chopped fresh parsley

In a heavy medium saucepan, melt butter over medium-high heat.

Add onion, garlic, thyme, and pepper, and sauté, stirring occasionally, for 5 minutes. Stir in mushrooms. Sprinkle with salt and cook, stirring occasionally, for 5 to 8 minutes until tender. Bring broth to a boil over high heat. Stir barley and hot broth into mushrooms. Bring to a boil. Reduce heat to low, cover, and simmer for 30 to 35 minutes until the barley is tender and most of the liquid is absorbed. Remove from heat and let stand, covered, for 5 minutes. Place in a warmed serving bowl. Garnish with chopped parsley. Serve.

Note: Pilafs are not always made with rice. It is a style of cooking that originated in the Mediterranean area.

Quinoa Timbales

Serves 6

1 tablespoon olive oil*
1 small onion, minced
1 teaspoon ground cumin
½ teaspoon ground cinnamon
¼ teaspoon turmeric
1 cup quinoa, rinsed
1 cup chicken broth
⅔ cup water
⅓ cup dried currants
¼ cup diced tomato
½ teaspoon salt
3 tablespoons minced fresh parsley
Sprigs of parsley

Heat oil in a heavy medium saucepan over medium-high heat. Add onion and sauté, stirring, until soft, about 5 minutes. Stir in cumin, cinnamon, and turmeric, and cook for 30 seconds. Add quinoa and cook, stirring, for 1 minute. Stir in broth, water, currants, tomato, and salt. Cover, reduce heat to medium-low and simmer for 15 minutes until the liquid is absorbed. Remove from heat. Let stand, covered, for 5 minutes. Stir in minced parsley.

Firmly pack one-sixth of quinoa mixture into a ½ cup ramekin or measuring cup. Invert, tapping gently, onto a platter. Make six. Garnish with sprigs of parsley. Serve.

Note: Quinoa is available at natural foods stores and specialty food sections of grocery stores.

Pad Thai

Sauce
¼ cup fish sauce*
¼ cup tamarind juice
¼ cup rice vinegar*
3 tablespoons granulated sugar
2 tablespoons soy sauce*
14 ounces dried rice noodles

Pad Thai
4 tablespoons peanut oil,* divided
8 ounces tofu,* cubed
3 eggs, well-beaten
4 cloves garlic, minced
1½ pounds shrimp, peeled, with tails on
1 teaspoon Thai hot chili sauce
4 cups bean sprouts*
1 cup chopped peanuts
1 bunch green onions sliced
¼ cup chopped Thai basil
¼ cup cilantro*
Lime wedges

In a medium bowl, combine fish sauce, tamarind juice, vinegar, sugar, and soy sauce, stirring until sugar is dissolved. Set aside. Soak noodles in hot water 15 minutes until slightly limp. Drain and set aside. Prepare and measure all of the other ingredients before beginning to cook.

Heat 3 tablespoons oil in a wok* or large skillet over medium-high heat. Add tofu and stir-fry until somewhat crispy on outside. Remove from wok and set aside. Add beaten eggs. Swirl to coat bottom of pan, working up the sides to make a thin omelet. Cook until set. Roll up and place on cutting board. Cut into thin slices. Set aside.

Increase heat to high. Add remaining oil to wok. Working quickly, add garlic and shrimp and toss until shrimp are about halfway done. Add chili sauce and toss to combine. Add noodles and toss well. Add bean sprouts and cooked tofu, and toss. Add peanuts, green onions, basil, and cilantro and toss.

When shrimp is just cooked through, add sauce. Heat 30 seconds and remove from stove. Turn into large serving bowl. Garnish with shredded eggs and lime wedges. Serve.

Note: This can be made with chicken breast instead of shrimp or with just the tofu.

Udon with Peanut Ginger Pesto

Serves 6

Peanut Ginger Pesto
2 tablespoon minced crystallized ginger*
1 to 2 jalapeño peppers, minced
4 cloves garlic, minced
1 cup toasted peanuts, divided
1½ cups fresh basil
½ cup fresh cilantro* or mint
2 tablespoons peanut oil*
1 tablespoon sesame oil*
1 tablespoon fish sauce*
1 tablespoon rice vinegar*
1 tablespoon soy sauce*

Noodles
14 ounces fresh udon noodles
1 tablespoon peanut oil
8 ounces fresh green beans, or 4 ounces snow peas,* julienned
3 carrots julienned
8 ounces mixed mushrooms, thinly sliced

Place ginger, jalapeño, garlic, ½ cup peanuts, basil, and cilantro in a blender or food processor. Slowly add peanut oil while motor is running. Turn off motor, scrape down sides, and pulse until somewhat blended. Mix in sesame oil, fish sauce, vinegar, and soy sauce. Scrape into bowl and adjust flavorings and set aside. Chop remaining peanuts and set aside.

Bring 2 quarts water to a boil in a large pot. Add noodles and cook 2 to 4 minutes. Drain well. Add Peanut Ginger Pesto and toss to coat.

Heat oil in skillet over medium heat. Add green beans, carrots, and mushrooms. Sauté 5 minutes until almost tender but still firm. Add vegetables to noodles and mix lightly. Sprinkle with remaining peanuts and serve.

Szechuan Noodle Toss   *Serves 8*

2 tablespoons sesame oil,* divided
4 green onions, cut into 1-inch pieces
1 carrot sliced
1 red bell pepper, julienned
1 green bell pepper, julienned
1 (15-ounce) can baby corn,* drained
1 (8-ounce) can water chestnuts,* drained and sliced
8 ounces garden spirals or small pasta shells, cooked
¼ cup soy sauce*
2 tablespoons rice vinegar*
½ teaspoon crushed red pepper
1 teaspoon fresh ginger,* minced

Sauté green onions in 1 tablespoon sesame oil until tender about 1 minute. Add carrot and cook approximately 1 minute. Add peppers and cook another minute. Add corn and water chestnuts and cook until vegetables are tender. Combine cooked vegetables with pasta. Mix remaining oil, soy sauce, vinegar, red pepper, and ginger and pour over pasta and vegetables. Toss and serve. This may be served warm or at room temperature.

Colorful Pasta Salad

Serves 12

¼ pound Provolone cheese, cubed
¼ pound hard salami, cubed
¼ pound pepperoni, cubed
1 medium onion, diced
1 medium green bell pepper, diced
3 stalks celery, diced
6 fresh tomatoes, diced
1 (2¼-ounce) can sliced black olives, drained
1 (7-ounce) jar green olives, drained and sliced
1 pound small tricolor pasta, cooked

Dressing
1¼ cups vegetable oil
⅔ cup cider vinegar
1 tablespoon salt
1 tablespoon oregano
1 teaspoon coarsely ground black pepper

Mix dressing ingredients in a bowl. Pour over salad and toss until well-combined. Cover and chill for 4 to 6 hours.

Spaghetti Michi

Serves 4 to 6

A chunky vegetarian spaghetti sauce.

2 tablespoons olive oil*
2 cloves garlic, pressed
1 medium onion, coarsely chopped
1 (28-ounce) can whole tomatoes, including juice, coarsely
    chopped
½ cup red wine
1 pint fresh mushrooms, halved
1 large red bell pepper, halved and sliced
1 large yellow bell pepper, halved and sliced
2 teaspoons oregano
1 teaspoon basil
1 teaspoon thyme
Salt and freshly ground pepper to taste
1 pound spaghetti, cooked and drained

Sauté onion and garlic in olive oil until limp. Add tomatoes, wine, mushrooms, peppers, and spices. Simmer until peppers are limp. Serve over spaghetti in a bowl.

Variation: Add 2 pounds of Italian sausage for a non-vegetarian sauce.

Sauces, Condiments, and Da Kine

Béchamel Sauce *Serves 4*

1½ tablespoons butter
2½ tablespoons flour
1 cup milk, heated to boiling

Melt butter in a saucepan. Add flour and mix well. Cook mixture for 3 minutes. Add milk, stirring constantly, until mixture thickens, about 3 minutes.

Blender Hollandaise *Makes ⅔ cup*

3 large egg yolks
1 tablespoon fresh lemon juice
⅛ teaspoon cayenne
½ cup hot melted butter

Combine egg yolks, lemon juice, and cayenne in blender. Mix lightly, just to break yolks. Turn blender on high and gradually add butter in a steady stream. Blend on high for 60 seconds and turn off for 30 seconds. Repeat this process until sauce thickens to a consistency where it does not drip form the spoon.

Note: It is important that the butter be hot in order to cook yolks. On-off cycle may have to be repeated as many as 10 to 12 times.

Char Siu Sauce

Makes 1 cup

A tasty marinade for pork, spareribs, or chicken.

1 cup brown sugar
¼ cup soy sauce*
½ teaspoon sesame oil*
⅛ teaspoon Chinese Five Spice*
1 clove garlic, minced
2 teaspoons sherry
1 tablespoon hoisin sauce*
1 tablespoon red food coloring

Combine ingredients and mix well. Marinate meat overnight.

Note: Meat should bake in a foil lined broiler pan at 350°F. Bake ribs for 30 minutes, pork and chicken for one hour.

Sweet and Sour Sauce

Makes 2 cups

Great for barbecues or as a dip for won ton. *

5 tablespoons sugar
1 tablespoon cornstarch
3 tablespoons vinegar
2 tablespoons Worcestershire sauce
4 tablespoons catsup
1½ cups water

Combine ingredients in a saucepan and cook over moderate heat until thick. Serve warm as a dipping sauce or use to baste meat before grilling.

Teriyaki Sauce Marinade *Makes 2 cups*

Great for grilling, broiling, or barbecue.

> 1 cup soy sauce*
> ½ cup water
> ¼ cup mirin*
> ⅓ cup brown sugar
> ½ cup sugar
> 1 tablespoon minced garlic
> 1 tablespoon minced fresh ginger*

Combine ingredients in a saucepan and heat until the sugars dissolve. Cool marinade before using. This recipe makes enough to marinate 3 to 4 pounds of meat, ribs, or chicken.

Hawaiian Barbecue Sauce *Makes 6 cups*

Use for basting or marinating poultry, pork, or beef.

> 2 cups olive oil*
> 1 cup catsup
> 1 cup soy sauce*
> ½ cup brown sugar
> 2 tablespoons salt
> 1 cup chopped celery
> 1 cup chopped onion
> 3 cloves garlic, crushed
> 1 teaspoon minced fresh ginger*
> 1 tablespoon chili sauce

Mix all ingredients in a saucepan. Bring to a boil, stirring occasionally. Reduce heat and simmer for one hour.

Aunty Olive's Barbecue Sauce

Makes 3 cups

Great for grilling, broiling, or barbecue.

1 cup catsup
⅓ cup oyster sauce*
1 cup brown sugar
¾ cup soy sauce*
1 onion, minced

Combine ingredients and mix well. Marinate ribs or chicken for at least ½ hour, but preferably overnight.

Satay Sauce

Makes 1½ cups

A peanut dipping sauce for chicken, vegetables, or apples.

¾ cup chicken stock
1 cup regular or crunchy peanut butter
¼ cup ketjap manis*
¼ cup shallots or green onions, including some tops, chopped
3 cloves garlic, minced
1½ tablespoons brown sugar
2 tablespoons fresh lemon or lime juice
1 teaspoon chili pepper flakes
¼ teaspoon fresh ginger,* grated

In a saucepan, bring chicken stock to a boil. Add remaining ingredients and stir until smooth. Let cool to room temperature before serving.

Note: Sauce may be prepared up to 3 hours ahead. Cover and refrigerate. Bring sauce to room temperature before serving.

Sweet and Sour Sauce for Fish

Makes 1 cup

¼ cup sugar
2 teaspoons cornstarch
Dash salt
3 tablespoons cold water
2 tablespoons white vinegar
1 tablespoon soy sauce*
1 tablespoon dry white wine

Combine ingredients in a saucepan and cook over low heat until bubbly and thick, stirring frequently. Serve warm as a dipping sauce or use to baste fish before grilling.

Chili Pepper Water

Makes 12 ounces

8 to 12 ounces water
2 to 3 cloves garlic, crushed
6 to 8 Hawaiian chili peppers,* mashed

Combine ingredients. Store in a jar and refrigerate.

Hot Pepper Jelly

Makes 1 quart

3 medium sweet bell peppers
8 to 10 hot peppers
6½ cups sugar
1½ cups cider vinegar
1 bottle Certo

Discard seeds and veins of peppers. Put sweet peppers and hot peppers through a meat grinder with a fine blade. Drain juice and pack peppers into 1 cup and use juice to flood to the full cup level. Bring sugar, peppers, and vinegar to a hard boil. Set aside where it will keep hot for 15 to 20 minutes, stirring occasionally. Bring to a full boil again for 2 minutes and stir in Certo. Skim and stir repeatedly until slightly cool to keep peppers from floating. Pour in sterilized jars and seal.

Mango Chutney

Makes 12 (6-ounce) jars

This makes an excellent year-round gift.

  1 quart vinegar
  3 pounds brown sugar
  4 pounds half-ripe mangoes,* peeled and cubed
  2 tablespoons salt
  2 pounds raisins
  1 ounce small Hawaiian chili peppers* (6 to 8), seeded and
      minced
  4 ounces fresh ginger,* minced
  4 ounces garlic, minced

Boil vinegar and sugar for 5 minutes. Add mangoes and simmer until they are soft. Add remaining ingredients and simmer 1 to 1½ hours until fruit is glazed. Sterilize jelly jars, fill with chutney, and seal while hot with melted paraffin wax.

Note: For milder chutney, use fewer chili peppers.

Papaya Pineapple Marmalade

Makes 2½ quarts

Tasty on toast, a treat on vanilla ice cream.

10 cups chopped firm-ripe papaya*
1 cup shredded fresh pineapple*
1 orange
2 lemons
3 tablespoons grated fresh ginger*
½ teaspoon salt
5 to 7 cups sugar

Combine papaya and pineapple in large saucepan. Squeeze one cup of lemon-orange juice and grate all three citrus rinds. Add juice, grated rinds, ginger, and salt. Bring to a boil and continue boiling (moderately) for 30 minutes. Add 5 cups sugar and taste for flavor. Add more if desired. Cook another 30 minutes, stirring frequently to avoid burning. Pour into sterilized jars.

Note: Do not store longer than 6 months.

Pineapple Salsa

Makes 2 cups

½ fresh pineapple,* cut into ¼- inch cubes
2 tomatoes, seeded, cut into ¼-inch cubes
½ medium Maui onion,* cut into ¼-inch cubes
¼ cup Chinese parsley,* chopped
½ teaspoon garlic, minced
1 jalapeño pepper, seeded and minced
1 teaspoon coriander seed, crushed
¾ teaspoon cumin
½ teaspoon salt

Mix all ingredients together. Cover and chill for at least one hour. Serve with grilled chicken or fish.

Pineapple Peppercorn Relish

Makes about 4 cups

3½ cups fresh pineapple,* diced
¾ cup minced red onion
¼ cup fresh lime juice
1½ tablespoons green peppercorns in brine, drained
Salt

In a bowl, combine pineapple, onion, lime juice, and peppercorns. Season with salt to taste. Cover and chill at least 2 hours before serving.

Note: Serve this with roasted poultry or fish.

Plum-Ginger Relish

Makes about 1 cup

6 red or black plums, peeled and diced
1 sweet red pepper, seeded and diced
2 green onions, thinly sliced
2 tablespoons minced red onion
2 tablespoons minced cilantro*
2 tablespoons minced pickled ginger*
3 tablespoons rice vinegar*
1 tablespoon granulated sugar
1 tablespoon safflower oil
1 tablespoon lime juice
1 teaspoon soy sauce*
½ teaspoon sesame oil*

Combine plums, pepper, green onions, red onion, cilantro, and ginger in a bowl. Stir to mix. Add vinegar, sugar, safflower oil, lime juice, soy sauce, and sesame oil. Stir to mix. Cover and chill several hours to blend flavors. Serve at room temperature.

Note: Great with grilled meat, fish or poultry. Can be used as dipping sauce with potstickers.

Sambal Cerise

Makes about 4 cups

1 large 'Ewa Sweet or Maui onion,* thinly sliced
2 cups fresh cherries, pitted and finely chopped
1 tablespoon packed brown sugar
⅓ cup fresh lime juice
4 small fresh hot red chilies

Caution: Wear rubber gloves to prepare hot chili or thoroughly wash hands after handling and do not touch your eyes.

Place onion and cherries in a medium non-reactive bowl. Sprinkle with sugar and lime juice and stir to mix. Cut each chili in half lengthwise. Add the seeds from one chili to bowl. Discard remaining seeds. Julienne each chili and add to bowl. Stir to mix. Cover and let stand at least 1 hour before serving. When off season, try using a mixture of chopped dried sweet cherries, dried sweetened cranberries, and golden raisins in place of the fresh cherries. Soak 10 minutes in 1¼ cups warm berry juice to plump.

Note: Serve as a condiment to poultry or pork.

Seasoning Salt

Makes 30 ounces

1 (26-ounce) box salt
2 to 4 tablespoons cayenne
2 tablespoons garlic powder
2 tablespoons chili powder

Combine ingredients and store in a tightly covered container.

Five-Spice Apples

Makes about 2 cups

2 tablespoons vegetable oil
1 small onion, finely diced
3 Granny Smith apples, peeled, cored, and diced
1½ teaspoons Chinese Five Spice* powder
1 tablespoon packed brown sugar
1 cup apple juice
Salt and black pepper
1 tablespoon butter

Heat oil in a medium skillet over medium heat and swirl to coat the bottom of the pan. Add onion and sauté, stirring occasionally, until golden, about 8 to 10 minutes. Add apples with five-spice powder and sugar, stirring to mix. Sauté a few minutes, then stir in juice. Season with salt and pepper to taste. Cook 10 to 12 minutes until liquid is reduced by half. The apples should retain their shape and some liquid should remain in the pan. Do not overcook. Stir in butter and adjust seasonings to taste. Serve warm.

Note: A nice condiment for grilled meat. Try substituting li hing mui for five-spice powder.

Boiled Peanuts

Makes 1 pound

1 pound raw peanuts in shell
½ cup Hawaiian rock salt *
3 to 4 star anise*
1 teaspoon sugar

Place peanuts in a pot and cover with water. Add rock salt, star anise, and sugar. Bring to a boil, cover and simmer for 1½ hours. Drain. Refrigerate.

Note: If these appear to be too salty at first, let them sit before serving.

Pink Onion Relish

2 cups water
1½ teaspoons white vinegar
1 large red onion, thinly sliced
1½ teaspoons vinegar
1 tablespoon salad oil
½ teaspoon mustard seed
¼ teaspoon cumin seed
Salt to taste

Bring water and vinegar to a boil in a small saucepan. Add the red onion and boil 2 to 3 minutes. Make sure the onions are immersed in the liquid. Drain and cool onions. Mix the cooled onions with the vinegar, salad oil, mustard seed, cumin seed, and salt. Serve with Vegetarian Chili.

Lūʻau

Poke Aku

Serves 20

A fresh raw fish flavored with seaweed and kukui nut (ʻinamona) which is served as a side dish or a pūpū.

> 5 pounds fresh aku*
> 3 pounds chopped limu kohu* or manuea Hawaiian rock salt*
>   to taste
> 3 to 4 tablespoons ʻinamona*

Skin the fish and cut into 1-inch cubes. Combine with remaining ingredients. Chill and serve.

Note: Fresh swordfish squid or octopus may be substituted. Must be fresh.

Variation: Korean style poke may be made using 3 to 5 seeded chopped Hawaiian chili peppers, 1 bunch chopped green onions, 2 tablespoons toasted sesame seeds, 1 tablespoon sesame oil, and 2 tablespoons soy sauce. Adjust to taste.

Lomi Lomi Salmon

Serves 20

This is the salad at a poi supper or lūʻau.

1 pound salted salmon
4 pounds tomatoes, finely chopped
2 medium Maui onions,* finely chopped
1 cup crushed ice
1 bunch green onions, finely chopped

Soak salmon in water for 2 to 3 hours, changing water several times. Drain and remove skin, bones, and white strings. Shred with spoon or fingers into small pieces. Place salmon, tomatoes, and onions into a bowl. Refrigerate until well-chilled. Top with thin layer of cracked ice one hour before serving. Just before serving, add green onions.

Note: If unsalted salmon is used, rub salmon with rock salt and let stand overnight. Rinse completely and soak in water 1 hour or more, changing water 2 to 3 times.

Pipikaula

Pipikaula* is Hawaiian beef jerky.

  4 pounds flank steak or brisket
  ⅓ cup red Hawaiian salt* or rock salt
  ¼ cup water
  ½ cup soy sauce*
  2 tablespoons brown sugar
  2 cloves garlic, minced
  1 tablespoon vegetable oil
  Soy sauce

Slice meat across the grain ¼-inch thick and 6 to 8 inches long. Sprinkle with salt. Drizzle with water and let stand for 1 hour. Mix soy sauce, brown sugar, garlic, and oil. Marinate meat overnight. Lay meat slices on a rack over a baking pan. Dry the meat in hot sun for one day, turning occasionally. Brown meat over a charcoal fire or fry in a pan in oil. Drizzle meat with soy sauce and serve.

Poi

Poi is a starch that is made from the taro plant. Although it may taste bland, poi takes on the flavor of the other foods.

7 pounds poi*
1 to 2 cups water

Use fresh, 1 or 2 day old poi. (Freeze-dried poi or bottled poi maybe used although flavor is more bland.) Turn bag inside out and squeeze poi into a mixing bowl. Gradually add water, mixing and squeezing with hands until smooth. Consistency is like a thick paste. Cover bowl and keep in cool place. Serve at room temperature.

Note: Each day it sits, it becomes more sour. If refrigerated, it will not sour as fast but must be covered with a layer of water. Mix with more water when ready to serve as poi will harden when cold.

Green Onions with Rock Salt

Serves 20

*Delicious with poi.** *

> 20 green onions
> 3 to 4 tablespoons Hawaiian rock salt*
> Hawaiian chili pepper* (optional)

Trim onions until each is about 6 to 8 inches long with white lower stem and some green top. Serve on square of ti leaf with ½ to 1 teaspoon rock salt on the side for "dipping." A fresh small Hawaiian chili pepper may also be served.

Note: Save remaining onion tops for use in Lomi Lomi Salmon (see page 189).

Chicken or Squid Lū'au
Serves 20

7 whole coconuts or 6 cups frozen coconut milk*
5 to 6 pounds chicken thighs or 5 to 6 pounds cooked squid
4 teaspoons salt
6 cups water
9 pounds taro leaves*

Pierce eyes of coconuts, drain coconut water into a bowl and set aside. Crack coconut open, remove white meat and grate. Pour 4 cups of reserved coconut water (add tap water if necessary to equal 4 cups) over grated coconut meat and let stand 15 minutes. Squeeze coconut meat and juice through 2 thicknesses of wet cheese cloth into a bowl. Set aside.

Place chicken in pot, add 3 teaspoons salt and 3 cups water and simmer uncovered until tender. Remove bones and cut chicken into 1-inch pieces and set aside. Cut squid in ½-inch pieces.

Wash taro leaves, remove stem, and strip tough part of rib. Place leaves, 3 cups water, and 1 teaspoon salt in a deep saucepan. Simmer for 1 hour. Change water and cook 1 hour more until bitter "sting" is out of leaves. Squeeze out excess water. Add drained chicken or squid and coconut milk to cooked taro leaves. Heat thoroughly and serve immediately. Adjust flavor with additional salt.

Chicken with Long Rice   *Serves 20*

This can be served as a main dish with steaming hot rice.

5 pounds chicken thighs
12 cups water
1 to 2 inches fresh ginger,* crushed
2 tablespoons Hawaiian rock salt*
2 cloves garlic, crushed (optional)
20 ounces long rice*
1 bunch green onions, chopped
Garnish: chopped green onions

Cover chicken with water. Add ginger, half the rock salt, and garlic and simmer 45 minutes or until tender. Cool.

Bone chicken and cut into bite-size pieces. Reserve broth. Remove ginger and discard. Add long rice to reserved broth and let stand ½ hour.

Remove long rice and cut into 4-inch lengths. Return long rice to broth. Add green onions, remaining rock salt, and chicken. Bring to boil and simmer 15 to 20 minutes. Add additional salt if desired.

Chicken long rice will be moist with a bit of broth as a sauce. Garnish with chopped onion.

Note: If made the day ahead, add a little extra chicken broth before reheating as the long rice will absorb existing broth.

Easy Chicken Lū'au

Can be used as an easy recipe for chicken lū'au in place of taro leaves and fresh coconut.

16 chicken thighs
1 teaspoon salt
6 pounds frozen leaf spinach
2 (12-ounce) cans frozen coconut milk*

Simmer chicken in salted water for 45 minutes or until tender. Bone, cut into bite-size pieces, and set aside. Thaw spinach, squeeze out excess water, add chicken and coconut milk. Heat until cooked through but do not boil. Serve hot.

Kālua Pig

Depending on the size of the puaʻa (pig), a suitable hole is dug in the ground. Hard wood is laid in the pit and is covered with river rounded lava rocks (which do not explode when heated). The wood is lit and the rocks are then heated for several hours until red hot. In the meantime, the pig is cleaned and the cavity rubbed with Hawaiian rock salt*. It is then placed on a large piece of chicken wire which is also used as a carrier. When the rocks are hot, some of them are placed in the cavity of the pig. The remaining rocks are covered with banana and ti leaves*. The pig is then lowered into the imu onto the bed of leaves. Bananas, sweet potatoes, or fish pre-wrapped in ti leaves are then added. Everything is then covered with another heavy layer of banana and ti leaves which are topped with a heavy layer of wet burlap bags, and finally the loose dirt. It is then hosed down but NOT SOAKED. If any steam escapes during cooking, more dirt is added. For a 100-pound pig cooking time would be approximately 6 hours.

At the appointed time, the imu is uncovered and care is taken that no dirt is dropped on the food. The pig is now carefully lifted out by the wire mesh and the rocks are removed from its cavity by the very adept hands of the imu workers. They place their bare hands in a pail of cold water, reach in and remove each hot rock, toss it aside, and redunk the heads to repeat the process. The pig is then carved and the meat shredded by hand.

Oven Kālua Pork

Oven Kālua Pork is a convenient substitute for pig from the imu. This is so easy and delicious you may want to serve it for a roast pork dinner.

8 pounds pork butt
4 tablespoons Hawaiian rock salt*
5 to 6 tablespoons liquid smoke
6 to 8 ti leaves*

Preheat oven to 500°F. Rub rock salt and liquid smoke over pork. Wrap pork in leaves and then in heavy foil. Bake in covered pan for ½ hour. Reduce temperature to 325°F and cook for 3½ hours. Shred into pieces and serve with a little of its own juice.

Note: Banana leaves, taro leaves, or spinach leaves may be substituted for a slightly different flavor.

Laulau

A delicious neatly wrapped bundle of pork, beef, and fish wrapped in taro and ti leaves and served in place of kālua pig at a poi supper or lū'au.

> 1½ pounds salted butterfish* or salted salmon
> 2½ pounds beef brisket or bottom round
> 5 pounds pork butt
> 2 pounds pork belly (optional)
> 200 taro leaves* (10 per laulau)
> 60 ti leaves* (3 per laulau*)

Salted fish should be soaked for ½ hour before cutting, changing the water twice. Cut fish and beef into 1-inch cubes and pork into 1½ to 2-inch cubes. Set aside. Wash ti and taro leaves. Remove tough ribs from the back of all leaves with small sharp knife. Remove stems from taro leaves. Peeled taro leaf stems may be cooked in laulau. Set ti leaves aside.

Assemble each laulau as follows: Place 10 taro leaves in a stack. In the middle of each place a piece of fish, beef, pork, and pork belly. Fold leaves to middle to make a neatly wrapped bundle.

Place 2 ti leaves across each other to make an "X." Place taro bundle on "X" with folded side down. Bring ends of one ti leaf together, closing tightly over bundle with ends standing up. Bring ends of second ti leaf and close in same manner to ensure total coverage of the bundle. Stems and ends should all be standing up. Holding bundle tightly with one hand, split stem of third ti leaf into two lengths with other hand. This will be your tie. Wind stem ties around the stems and ends several times, securing tightly and finish with a knot. Cut remaining stems and ends 3 to 4 inches above knot for a neat package. Steam* laulau for a minimum of 4 hours.

Mullet Baked in Ti Leaves   *Serves 20*

4 pounds mullet *
¼ cup Hawaiian rock salt*
5 ti leaves*

Preheat oven to 350°F. Clean fish and sprinkle with salt. Lay fish lengthwise on a ti leaf. Wrap fish with additional leaves until covered. Tie ends with string or piece of stem. Place on jelly roll pan and bake uncovered for 30 to 40 minutes. Transfer to platter. Cut open ti leaves and serve.

Note: Add onions if desired.

Haupia

Traditional dessert served with lū'au food.

    12 ounces frozen coconut milk*
    1½ cups water
    ½ cup plus 2 tablespoons sugar
    ½ cup plus 2 tablespoons cornstarch

Combine all ingredients in saucepan. Stir over medium heat until thickened. Lower heat and cook for ten minutes, stirring constantly to avoid lumping or burning. Pour into 8 x 8-inch dish and chill until set. Cut haupia* into squares.

Note: May be topped with crushed pineapple, sliced peaches, or sliced mango.

Beverages

Tropical Fruit Cooler   *Makes 1½ gallons*

6 cups water
4 cups sugar
1 (48-ounce) can pineapple* juice
6 bananas
1 (6-ounce) can frozen orange juice concentrate, thawed
½ cup fresh lemon juice
1 gallon ginger ale
½ gallon club soda
Garnish: orange slices and lemon slices

Boil sugar in water to dissolve. Let cool. Blend juices and bananas in a blender. Mix with sugar and water syrup and freeze in two blocks. Thirty to forty-five minutes before serving, pour half ginger ale over frozen mixture in punch bowl. Add remaining ginger ale and club soda. Garnish and serve.

O.C.C. Iced Tea

Makes 1 gallon

½ gallon water
12 tea bags
3 sprigs fresh mint
1⅔ cups sugar
12 ounces pineapple* juice
6 ounces lemon juice
Garnish: Mint sprigs and pineapple spears

Bring water to a boil and steep tea bags and mint. Remove mint after 3 minutes. Continue to steep tea until it is very dark. Remove tea bags. While tea is still warm, add sugar and juices, stirring to dissolve sugar. Pour into a gallon container, adding enough water to fill to the gallon level. Chill. Serve iced with mint sprigs and pineapple spears.

Oahu Country Club
Honolulu, Hawai'i

White Sangria

Serves 6

4 cups dry white wine
¾ cup Cointreau
½ cup sugar
1 (10-ounce) bottle club soda, chilled
1 small bunch green grapes
1 sliced orange
1 sliced lemon
1 sliced lime
Garnish: Green apple wedges dipped in lemon juice

Mix white wine, Cointreau, and sugar and chill. Just before serving, stir in the club soda, adding grapes, orange, lemon, and lime slices. For each serving, garnish glass with an apple wedge.

Blue Hawai'i

Makes 1 drink

Blue Curaçao gives this drink its unique color.

2½ ounces pineapple* juice
1 teaspoon Orgeat syrup
1 ounce Blue Curaçao
½ ounce vodka

Combine the ingredients. Fill a 12-ounce goblet with shaved ice and pour mixture over ice.

Al Hong
Trader Vic's Restaurant
Honolulu, Hawai'i

Hotel Hāna Maui ChiChi   *Serves 1*

2 cups crushed ice
1½ ounces vodka
6 ounces pineapple* juice
2 ounces thick coconut syrup*

Blend in blender. For a frozen chichi, blend longer. Serve in a tall glass.

Hotel Hāna Maui
Hāna, Maui

Beachcomber   *Serves 1*

1 fluid ounce gin
6 fluid ounces pineapple* juice
1 fluid ounce Triple Sec
¾ cup ice
Fresh pineapple* chunk

Combine gin, pineapple juice, Triple Sec, and ice in a blender. Purée until smooth. Pour into a cocktail glass. Garnish with pineapple and serve.

Pink Plumeria

Serves 4

1 cup cracked ice
7½ fluid ounces dry London-type gin
Juice of 2 limes
1 tablespoon granulated sugar
Grenadine
Fresh pineapple* chunks
Bamboo skewers

Put ice in cocktail shaker. Add gin, lime juice, and sugar. Shake vigorously for 15 seconds. Strain into chilled cocktail glasses. Add 6 drops of grenadine to each. Skewer pineapple chunks on bamboo. Garnish drinks with pineapple and serve.

Lāna'i Fizz

Makes 1 gallon

1 (12-ounce) can frozen orange juice concentrate, thawed
1 (12-ounce) can frozen pineapple* juice concentrate, thawed
¼ cup lemon juice
2 bottles champagne, chilled
1 liter lemon-lime soda, chilled
Garnish: orange slices

Mix juices together and chill. Just before serving, add champagne and soda. Stir and garnish with floating orange slices.

Li Hing Mui Margarita

Li hing mui* powder
Granulated sugar
1 lime, cut into wedges
2 fluid ounces fresh lime juice
4 fluid ounces Triple Sec
8 fluid ounces tequila
3 cups ice cubes

Mix equal parts of li hing mui powder with sugar. Run one lime wedge around edges of margarita glasses to moisten. Dip glass edges in li hing mui mixture and set aside. Combine lime juice, Triple Sec, tequila, and ice in blender and purée until smooth. Fill prepared glasses. Garnish with lime and serve.

An alternate method is to combine lime juice, Triple Sec, tequila, and crushed ice in shaker and shake vigorously for 30 seconds before pouring into rimmed glasses.

Wicked Mai Tai Punch

Makes 2½ to 3 quarts

38 ounces dark Jamaican rum
7 ounces Curaçao
5 ounces Orgeat syrup
10 ounces rock candy syrup
25 ounces lemon juice
3 small limes, juiced
3 to 4 cups sugar
Garnish: Mint sprigs and pineapple* spears

Mix the ingredients together. Serve over ice in a punch bowl or over crushed ice in a glass. Garnish with mint and pineapple spears.

Buzz's Golden Coyne

Serves 1

¼ ounce white rum
¼ ounce Tuaca
1 ounce milk
2 scoops ice cream
Garnish: Whipped cream

Blend first three ingredients in a blender. Pour mixture into an 8-ounce tulip or wine glass. Top with scoops of ice cream and a dollop of whipped cream.

Bobby Lou Schneider
Buzz's Original Steak House-Mōʻiliʻili
Honolulu, Hawaiʻi

Mango Daiquiri

Serves 2

1 cup chopped peeled fresh ripe mango*
3 fluid ounces dark rum
1 tablespoon granulated sugar
1 fluid ounce Rose's lime juice
2 cups cracked ice

Combine mango with rum, sugar, lime juice, and cracked ice in a blender. Purée, scraping down the sides occasionally, until mixture is smooth and frozen. Pour into two stemmed cocktail glasses and serve.

Pink Palace

Serves 1

4 ounces pineapple* juice
½ ounce lemon juice
1 ounce half-and-half
1½ ounces cream of coconut
1 ounce Grand Marnier
Dash Grenadine
Handful of ice
Garnish: Pineapple, cherry and orchid

Combine ingredients and whirl in blender. Pour into a 22-ounce glass half filled with crushed ice. Garnish.

Royal Hawaiian Hotel
Honolulu, Hawai'i

Kona Coffee Punch

Makes 5 to 6 quarts

4 quarts strong Kona coffee,* chilled
1 quart whipping cream
5 tablespoons sugar
5 teaspoons vanilla
2 quarts vanilla ice cream
4 ounces chocolate syrup (optional)
1 cup coffee liqueur (optional)
Garnish: chocolate shavings

Whip cream until stiff peaks form, gradually adding sugar and vanilla. Combine coffee, chocolate syrup, and coffee liqueur. Spoon ice cream into a large punch bowl and carefully pour in chilled coffee mixture. Top with mounds of whipped cream. Garnish with chocolate shavings and serve.

Kona coffee is one of the most sought after origin coffees in the world. Grown on the west coast of the "Big Island" of Hawai'i, these coffee beans benefit from a unique cloud cover that appears around two o'clock every afternoon, just in time to protect the delicate trees from the intense heat of the tropical sun. Its medium body, fair acidity, and wine-like tones produce a rich aroma.

Desserts

Banana Cake Wai'alae Iki   *Serves 16*

¼ cup butter, softened
1⅓ cups sugar
2 eggs
1 teaspoon vanilla
2 cups flour
1 teaspoon baking powder
1 teaspoon baking soda
¾ teaspoon salt
1 (8-ounce) carton sour cream
1 cup mashed bananas
1 cup chopped pecans

Preheat oven to 350°F. Grease and flour a 9 x 13-inch pan. Set aside. In a large mixing bowl, cream butter and sugar until light and fluffy. Add eggs and vanilla and blend thoroughly. Sift together flour, baking powder, baking soda, and salt. Add to creamed mixture alternately with sour cream, beginning and ending with dry ingredients. Stir in bananas and pecans. Spread batter evenly over bottom of pan and bake 40 to 45 minutes. Cool and frost with Cream Cheese Frosting.

Cream Cheese Frosting
8 ounces cream cheese, softened
¼ cup melted butter
1 teaspoon vanilla
1 (16-ounce) box powdered sugar

Combine all ingredients and blend well.

Guava Cake

2 cups sugar
1 cup butter
4 eggs
3 cups flour
¾ teaspoon nutmeg
1¼ teaspoons baking soda
¼ teaspoon ground cloves
¼ teaspoon cinnamon
1 cup frozen guava* juice concentrate
½ cup guava juice
¼ teaspoon red food coloring

Preheat oven to 350°F. Cream sugar and butter until fluffy. Add eggs one at a time and beat well. Sift dry ingredients in a separate bowl. Mix guava concentrate and guava juice. Add dry ingredients and liquid alternately to creamy mixture until well-blended. Pour into greased and floured 9 x 13 x 2-inch pan. Bake for 30 minutes. Cool and frost with Butter Cream Frosting or Cream Cheese Frosting (see page 213).

Butter Cream Frosting
1 cup butter, softened
¼ teaspoon salt
2½ cups powdered sugar
5 tablespoons whipping cream
1 teaspoon vanilla

Combine butter, salt, powdered sugar, and whipping cream. Beat with an electric mixer until very smooth and creamy. Stir in vanilla.

Note: Additional powdered sugar may be added to obtain desired consistency. **Variations:** Add 1 tablespoon instant coffee or cocoa and 2 to 3 tablespoons crème de cacao.

Apple Spice Cake

Serves 14 to 16

Just like Grandma used to make.

½ cup brown sugar
1 cup sugar
½ cup shortening
2 eggs
1 cup buttermilk
1 teaspoon baking soda
½ teaspoon salt
1½ teaspoons cinnamon
2½ cups flour
1 teaspoon vanilla
3 cups apples, peeled and diced

Preheat oven to 350°F. Grease and flour a 9 x 13-inch baking pan. Cream sugars and shortening. Add eggs, buttermilk, baking soda, salt, cinnamon, flour, and vanilla and mix well. Fold in apples. Pour into prepared pan. Sprinkle topping over batter and bake for 50 to 55 minutes.

Topping
⅓ cup brown sugar
⅓ cup sugar
1 teaspoon cinnamon
½ cup walnuts, chopped

Combine brown sugar, sugar, and cinnamon and blend well. Add walnuts and toss to coat evenly.

Note: Add 1 tablespoon vinegar or lemon juice to regular milk to sour it if buttermilk is not available.

Coconut Cake

Serves 16

¾ cup butter
2 cups sugar
¾ cup grated fresh coconut*
2½ cups flour
4 teaspoons baking powder
1 cup coconut water* (make up difference with milk)
4 egg whites

Preheat oven to 350°F. Butter and flour three 8-inch or two 9-inch round pans. Cream butter and sugar until light and fluffy. Add grated coconut. Sift flour and baking powder. Alternately add flour and coconut water to creamed mixture. Beat egg whites until they form soft peaks. Fold into batter. Pour batter into pans. Bake for 20 to 30 minutes. Top with Coconut Frosting.

Coconut Frosting
1 cup sugar
⅓ cup boiling water
¼ teaspoon cream of tartar
2 teaspoons light corn syrup
2 egg whites
1 teaspoon vanilla
2 cups grated coconut*

In a double boiler, mix sugar, water, cream of tartar and corn syrup. Stir until sugar dissolves. Add the egg whites and remove from heat. Beat mixture on high speed for exactly 5 minutes. Return to heat. Keep water simmering and heat mixture exactly 4 minutes longer. Add the vanilla. Frost each layer and sprinkle with coconut.

Note: The frosting will keep in an airtight container in the refrigerator up to 1 week.

Hawaiian Carrot Cake   *Serves 12 to 14*

3 eggs
2 cups sugar
1½ cups vegetable oil
2 teaspoons vanilla
1 (7-ounce) can crushed pineapple,* undrained
2 cups grated carrots
3 cups cake flour
½ teaspoon allspice
1 teaspoon baking powder
1 teaspoon baking soda
1 teaspoon salt
1 teaspoon cinnamon
1 teaspoon nutmeg
1 cup chopped macadamia nuts*
1 tablespoon powdered sugar

Preheat oven to 350°F. In a large mixing bowl, cream eggs, sugar, and oil. Continue beating and add vanilla, crushed pineapple, and carrots. Combine dry ingredients and sift 3 times. Slowly beat dry mixture into batter. Add nuts and blend thoroughly. Pour batter into greased and floured Bundt pan. Bake for 1 hour and 15 minutes. While warm, dust with powdered sugar or cool and frost with Cream Cheese Frosting (see page 213).

Deluxe Carrot Cake

This three-layer cake is as delicious as it is beautiful.

2 cups flour
2 cups sugar
2 teaspoons baking soda
1 teaspoon salt
2 teaspoons cinnamon
4 eggs
1 cup vegetable oil
4 cups carrots, grated
¾ cup macadamia nuts,* chopped

Preheat oven to 350°F. Combine flour, sugar, baking soda, salt, and cinnamon. Set aside. In a large bowl, beat eggs until foamy. Slowly beat in oil. Add flour mixture gradually, beating until smooth. Mix in carrots and nuts. Pour into 3 greased and floured 9-inch round cake pans. Bake for 25 minutes. Cool for 10 minutes before removing from pans. Then cool completely on racks. Frost with Coconut Cream Cheese Frosting.

Coconut Cream Cheese Frosting
4 tablespoons butter or margarine, divided
2 cups coconut*
8 ounces cream cheese
2 teaspoons milk
3½ cups powdered sugar, sifted
½ teaspoon vanilla

Melt 2 tablespoons butter in a skillet. Add coconut and cook, stirring constantly over low heat, until golden brown. Cool on paper towels. Cream remaining 2 tablespoons butter and cream cheese. Add milk and sugar alternately, beating well after each addition. Add vanilla and stir in 1¾ cups of the prepared coconut. Frost each layer and sprinkle top with remaining coconut.

Clem's Chocolate Cake
Serves 16

Chocoholics will enjoy the speed with which this rich cake can be prepared.

½ cup margarine
4 heaping tablespoons cocoa
1 cup water
2 cups flour
2 cups sugar
½ cup buttermilk
1 teaspoon baking soda
2 eggs, lightly beaten
1 teaspoon vanilla
1 teaspoon cinnamon

Preheat oven to 425°F. Melt margarine in saucepan. Add cocoa and water and bring to a boil. Pour over flour and sugar. Combine buttermilk and soda and add with eggs, vanilla, and cinnamon. Mix well and pour into a 9 x 13-inch pan. Bake for 20 minutes and frost immediately with Fudge Frosting.

Fudge Frosting
½ cup margarine
4 tablespoons cocoa
6 tablespoons milk
1 (16-ounce) box powdered sugar
1 teaspoon vanilla
1 cup chopped nuts

Combine margarine, cocoa, and milk in saucepan and bring to a boil. Remove from heat and beat in sugar, vanilla, and nuts. Pour over Clem's Chocolate Cake while hot.

Lavender Coffee Cake   *Serves 8 to 10*

⅓ cup macadamia nut halves
¾ cup golden raisins
3 tablespoons sweet Marsala or sherry
2¼ cups all-purpose flour
1½ teaspoons baking powder
½ teaspoon baking soda
¼ teaspoon salt
1 tablespoon grated lemon zest
3 eggs
½ cup olive oil*
½ cup honey, divided
¾ cup plain yogurt
⅓ cup fresh lemon juice
1 tablespoon dried lavender flowers

Heat oven to 350°F. Butter and flour a 9-inch springform pan. Set aside. Spread nuts in a baking pan and place in center of oven. Heat 3 to 5 minutes, shaking frequently, until fragrant and the color deepens. Remove from pan. Set aside and let cool. Put raisins in a small bowl, sprinkle with Marsala, and stir lightly. Let stand for 10 minutes. Stir together flour, baking powder, baking soda, salt, and lemon zest. Set aside.

In a large bowl, beat eggs with a whisk until well-blended. Stir in oil, ¼ cup honey, and yogurt. Add soaked raisins with any liquid and dry ingredients. Stir with wooden spoon just until blended and almost smooth. Pour batter into prepared pan. Smooth top with spatula. Bake in center of oven 25 to 30 minutes, until a toothpick inserted in center comes out clean.

Combine remaining ¼ cup honey, lemon juice, and lavender in a small saucepan. Bring to a boil over medium heat, stirring occasionally. Remove from heat. Let cool.

When cake tests done, place pan on wire rack and poke the top all over with a wooden skewer or toothpick. Brush with half of the glaze. Let cool 10 minutes.

Remove sides of pan from coffee cake, invert cake onto rack, and remove bottom of pan. Poke bottom of cake with skewer. Brush with remaining glaze. Place inverted serving plate on bottom of cake. Turn cake upright. Sprinkle with toasted nuts. Cut into wedges and serve.

Fresh Banana Cheesecake

Crust
1½ cups quick-cooking rolled oats
½ cup pecans, finely chopped
½ cup brown sugar
⅓ cup butter, melted

Preheat oven to 350°F. Stir together oats, pecans, brown sugar, and butter until well-combined. Press firmly into the bottom and sides of a 9-inch springform pan. Bake for 18 minutes or until golden brown. Cool.

Filling
1 pound cream cheese, at room temperature
1 cup ripe bananas, mashed
¾ cup sugar
2 teaspoons lemon juice
4 eggs

Topping
1 cup sour cream
2 tablespoons sugar
1 teaspoon vanilla
Garnish: banana slices

Preheat oven to 350°F. Beat together cream cheese, bananas, ¾ cup sugar, and lemon juice until well-blended. Add eggs, one at a time, beating well after each addition. Pour into crust. Bake for 40 minutes.

While cake is baking, prepare sour cream topping by mixing together sour cream, 2 tablespoons sugar, and vanilla until well-blended.

Remove cheesecake from oven and top with sour cream mixture. Return to oven and bake for 10 minutes more.

Cool slightly. Loosen cake from sides of pan. Cool to room temperature. Refrigerate uncovered overnight. Garnish with banana slices before serving.

White Chocolate Cake   *Serves 12 to 14*

½ pound white chocolate, grated
1 cup butter
2 cups sugar
4 eggs, separated
2½ cups flour
1 teaspoon baking powder
½ teaspoon salt
1 cup buttermilk
1 cup chopped pecans
1 cup flaked coconut*
1 teaspoon vanilla

Preheat oven to 325°F. In double boiler, melt chocolate and remove from heat. In a large bowl, cream butter and sugar until light and fluffy. Add egg yolks and beat well. Add chocolate. Sift flour, baking powder, and salt together. Add to above mixture alternately with buttermilk. Mix well. Add pecans, coconut, and vanilla. Beat egg whites until stiff and fold into batter. Pour into ungreased tube pan and bake for 1 hour and 10 minutes.

Note: Do not allow water to come to a full boil when melting chocolate; steam changes chocolate consistency.

Mocha Cheesecake

Serves 10 to 12

1 cup graham cracker crumbs
¼ cup butter
2 tablespoons sugar
½ teaspoon cinnamon
2 tablespoons instant coffee
¼ cup hot water
1½ pounds cream cheese, at room temperature
¾ cup sugar
3 large eggs
8 ounces semi-sweet chocolate
2 tablespoons whipping cream
1 cup sour cream
¼ cup coffee liqueur
2 teaspoons vanilla
Garnish: chocolate shavings

Preheat oven to 350°F. Butter sides of 8-inch springform pan. Combine graham cracker crumbs, butter, sugar, and cinnamon. Press evenly onto bottom of pan. Chill while making filling.

Dissolve instant coffee in hot water. Set aside to cool.

Beat cream cheese until smooth. Add sugar gradually, mixing until well-blended. Add eggs one at a time, beating well after each addition. Melt chocolate with whipping cream over low heat, stirring constantly. Add to cheese mixture, blending well. Mix in sour cream, then cooled coffee and liqueur. Beat in vanilla. Pour over prepared crust.

Bake for 45 minutes or until sides are slightly puffed. Center will be still a bit soft, but will firm up when chilled. Cool cake on rack. Refrigerate, uncovered, for at least 12 hours before serving. Garnish with chocolate shavings and serve.

Coconut Cheesecake *Serves 10 to 12*

Crust
1 cup graham cracker crumbs
¼ cup granulated sugar
3 tablespoons butter, melted
1½ cups shredded coconut*

Filling
2 pounds cream cheese, softened
1 cup granulated sugar
5 eggs
14 to 16 ounces canned cream of coconut, such as Coco Lopez
1 cup thick coconut milk*
¼ teaspoon salt
⅛ teaspoon grated lemon zest
1 teaspoon vanilla extract

Topping
3 tablespoons butter
¼ cup packed brown sugar
½ cup chopped macadamia nuts,* toasted

Heat oven to 375°F. In a small bowl, mix together graham cracker crumbs, sugar, and melted butter. Press onto bottom of a 10-inch springform pan. Bake 10 minutes. Remove from oven, sprinkle with coconut and cool. Reduce oven to 350°F.

In a large bowl, beat cream cheese until light. Add sugar and beat until blended. Add eggs, one at a time, beating just until combined. Stir in cream of coconut, coconut milk, salt, lemon zest, and vanilla. Blend well. Pour onto coconut sprinkled crust. Bake about 1 hour to 1 hour and 15 minutes, until cheesecake is set but moves just slightly when shaken. Top may crack.

Run a knife between side of pan and cheesecake to loosen edge. Remove to wire rack and let cool. Cover and chill several hours or overnight.

Release pan sides. Using a long spatula, loosen bottom and slide cheesecake onto serving plate. Melt butter and brown sugar over medium heat in a medium saucepan. Remove from heat and stir in macadamia nuts. Spread over cheesecake. Cut into wedges and serve.

Note: Cream of Coconut is a homogenized cream made from the meat of the coconut and blended with cane sugar to result in a smooth sweet coconut cream.

Okinawan Sweet Potato-Haupia Cheesecake

Serves 10 to 12

Crust
1½ cups graham cracker crumbs
¼ cup granulated sugar
3 tablespoons butter, melted

Filling
2 pounds cream cheese, softened
¾ cup granulated sugar
4 eggs
1 teaspoon vanilla extract
¼ teaspoon salt
3 cups cooked mashed Okinawan sweet potato

Haupia Topping
12 to 14 ounces canned thick coconut milk*
¾ cup granulated sugar
3 tablespoons cornstarch
3 tablespoons water
1 tablespoon vanilla extract

Heat oven to 350°F. In a small bowl, mix together graham cracker crumbs, sugar, and melted butter. Press onto bottom of a 10-inch springform pan. Bake 10 minutes. Remove to wire rack and let cool.

In a large bowl, beat cream cheese until light. Add sugar and beat until blended. Add eggs one at a time, beating just until combined. Stir in vanilla, salt, and mashed sweet potato until blended. Pour onto baked crust. Bake about 1 hour 15 minutes, until cheesecake is set but moves just slightly when shaken. Top may crack.

Remove to wire rack. Run a knife around inside edge of pan.

In saucepan, bring coconut milk and sugar to a boil, stirring frequently, over medium heat. Mix together cornstarch and water. Add to hot coconut milk, stirring until thickened. Remove from heat and stir in vanilla. Let stand 5 minutes, stirring occasionally before pouring onto cheesecake. Cover and refrigerate several hours or overnight to set. Run a knife between side of pan and cheesecake to loosen edge. Release pan sides. Using long spatula, loosen bottom and slide onto serving plate. Cut into wedges and serve.

Chocolate Cheesecake *Serves 8 to 10*

Crust
¾ cup graham cracker crumbs
5 tablespoons melted butter
2 tablespoons sugar
2 tablespoons grated semi-sweet chocolate

Combine ingredients and press firmly into the bottom of an 8 or 9-inch spring form pan. Chill while making filling.

Filling
3 eggs
1 cup sugar
24 ounces cream cheese, softened
12 (1-ounce) squares semi-sweet chocolate, grated
1 cup sour cream
¾ cup butter
1 teaspoon vanilla
1 cup chopped pecans
Garnish: whipped cream

Preheat oven to 325°F. Combine eggs and sugar and blend until light and creamy. Add softened cream cheese, blending until well-mixed.

In a double boiler combine chocolate, sour cream, butter, and vanilla. Simmer until chocolate is melted. Stir chocolate mixture into cheese mixture. Fold in pecans. Pour into spring form pan and bake for 2 hours or until center is firm.

Let cake cool on wire rack. Chill for 12 hours and serve with whipped cream.

"Never Fail" Pie Crust *Makes 2 (9-inch) crusts*

1¼ cups shortening
3 cups flour
1 egg, beaten
5 tablespoons water
1 tablespoon white vinegar
1 teaspoon salt

Cut shortening into flour. Mix egg with water, vinegar, and salt. Add to flour mixture and blend well. Let dough rest 5 minutes. Roll out and trim to fit pie plate.

Mango Pie

Serves 8

Hawaiian version of peach pie.

2 (8-inch) unbaked pie shells
3 cups peeled and sliced mangoes*
¼ to ½ cup sugar
2 tablespoons flour
⅛ teaspoon salt
1½ tablespoons lemon juice
½ teaspoon cinnamon
¼ teaspoon nutmeg
1 tablespoon butter

Preheat oven to 350°F. In large bowl, combine mangoes, sugar, flour, salt, lemon juice, cinnamon, and nutmeg. Pour mixture into pie shell. Lattice strips of the second pie shell over top of pie and dot with butter. Bake for 1 hour.

Note: Ripeness of mangoes will determine the amount of sugar needed. Use less sugar with riper mangoes.

Lemon Ribbon Pie

Serves 8

A cool and creamy summertime treat.

1 (9-inch) pie shell, baked
1 quart vanilla ice cream, softened
6 tablespoons butter
Zest of 1 lemon
⅓ cup lemon juice
⅛ teaspoon salt
1 cup plus 6 tablespoons sugar, divided
2 eggs
2 egg yolks
3 egg whites

Smooth half of the ice cream into the pie shell. Freeze. Melt butter in a saucepan over low heat. Add lemon zest, lemon juice, salt, and 1 cup sugar and mix well. Slightly beat eggs with egg yolks. Combine with lemon juice mixture and cook over low heat, beating constantly with a wire whisk until smooth, approximately 10 to 15 minutes. Let cool.

Spread ice cream with half of the lemon butter sauce and freeze until firm. Spread with the remaining ice cream and freeze. Top with remaining lemon butter sauce and freeze. Preheat oven to 475°F. Beat egg whites until they form soft peaks. Gradually beat in 6 tablespoons sugar until whites are thick and glossy. Spread meringue on the pie. Place on cookie sheet in oven and bake until lightly browned on top. Serve immediately.

Two Crust Banana Pie

Serves 8

2 (9-inch) unbaked pie shells
2½ cups bananas, cut into ¼-inch slices
1 cup pineapple* juice
½ cup sugar
3 tablespoons flour
1 teaspoon cinnamon
½ teaspoon nutmeg
Pinch salt
1 tablespoon butter
2 tablespoons milk

Preheat oven to 400°F. Soak bananas in pineapple juice for 20 to 30 minutes. Drain.

Combine dry ingredients and mix with bananas. Pour filling into pastry shell. Dot with butter and place top crust over filling. Seal and flute pastry edges, brush with milk, and cut slits. Bake for 30 to 35 minutes. Serve warm or cold with Pineapple Brandy Sauce (see page 264).

Pineapple Cream Cheese Pie

Serves 8

1 (9-inch) unbaked pie shell
⅓ cup sugar
1 tablespoon cornstarch
1 (9-ounce) can crushed pineapple,* undrained
8 ounces cream cheese, softened
½ cup sugar
½ teaspoon salt
2 eggs
½ cup milk
½ teaspoon vanilla
¼ cup chopped pecans

Preheat oven to 400°F. Blend sugar with cornstarch and add pineapple. Cook, stirring constantly, until the mixture is thick and clear. Cool.

Blend cream cheese with sugar and salt. Add eggs one at a time, stirring well after each addition. Blend in milk and vanilla. Spread the cooled pineapple mixture over the bottom of the pie shell. Pour in cream cheese mixture and sprinkle with pecans. Bake for 10 minutes, then reduce heat to 325°F and bake for an additional 50 minutes. Cool before serving.

Mango Lime Cream Pie

Serves 10 to 12

1½ cups graham cracker crumbs
4 tablespoons unsalted butter, softened
¼ cup fresh lime juice
1½ teaspoons unflavored powdered gelatin
12 ounces cream cheese, softened
½ cup confectioners' sugar
2¼ teaspoons grated lime zest
1 cup mango* purée
2 cups well-chilled heavy or whipping cream
2 firm ripe mangoes*

Heat oven to 350°F. Line bottom of a 10-inch springform pan with parchment paper and set aside. In a bowl, combine graham crackers with butter and mix well. Press firmly into bottom of the prepared pan and bake until firm, 10 to 15 minutes. Remove from oven and cool completely on a wire rack.

In a small saucepan, heat lime juice and gelatin over low heat until the gelatin dissolves, about 3 minutes. Remove from heat and let cool slightly.

In a large bowl, beat cream cheese until light and fluffy with electric mixer or by hand. Add sugar and lime zest and beat until well-blended. Add the softened gelatin and mango purée and mix to combine. In a bowl, whip the cream until soft peaks form. Using a rubber spatula, fold into the mango purée mixture and pour over crust, smoothing the top. Cover with plastic wrap and refrigerate at least 4 hours until firm. Peel mangoes, remove seed, and dice flesh. Cover and chill. Serve garnished with diced mango.

Macadamia Nut Pie

Serves 8

1 (9-inch) deep dish pie shell, unbaked
3 eggs
1 cup sugar
1½ tablespoons flour
⅓ cup melted butter
1 cup dark corn syrup
1⅓ cups macadamia nut bits*
1 teaspoon vanilla

Preheat oven to 400°F. Combine eggs, sugar, flour, butter, corn syrup, nuts, and vanilla. Pour into pie shell and bake for 15 minutes. Reduce temperature to 350°F and bake until golden brown an additional 40 to 45 minutes.

Apple Macadamia Nut Tart

Serves 8 to 10

¾ cup macadamia nut pieces
1¼ cups all-purpose flour
¾ cup plus 1 tablespoon granulated sugar divided
¾ cup butter, cut into small pieces, divided
1 egg yolk
3 eggs
2 to 3 Granny Smith apples
¼ cup liliko'i or apricot jam
2 tablespoons Cointreau

Heat oven to 325°F. Spread nuts in bottom of a small baking pan and bake until golden, about 5 to 8 minutes, watching carefully so nuts do not burn, shaking pan often. Pour from pan to a dish and let cool.

Keep oven on.

In a bowl, mix flour and 1 tablespoon sugar. Add ½ cup butter. Blend together with fork to form texture of fine sand. Add egg yolk, mixing until dough holds together. Gather and pat into a smooth ball. Place in a 9-inch tart pan with removable bottom. Working from center out, firmly press dough over bottom and up sides of pan. Set aside.

Put toasted macadamia nuts and remaining sugar in food processor. Pulse until nuts are finely ground. Add remaining butter and whole eggs and whirl until smooth. Set aside.

Peel, core, and slice apples ⅛-inch thick. Arrange apple slices, overlapping, neatly in tart pan. Drizzle with nut mixture. Bake 50 to 60 minutes until crust is browned and apples are tender.

Remove to wire rack and cool. Filling will be puffy then settle upon cooling.

In a small bowl, stir together jam and liqueur. Drizzle over cooling tart. Let sit at least 30 minutes before removing rim. Serve warm or cooled, cut into wedges.

Garden Café Coconut Shortbread Cookies

Makes 6 dozen

The Garden Café was founded in 1969. Excellent food and a pleasant atmosphere make lunching there a delightful experience.

¾ pound butter
¼ pound margarine
1 cup sugar
1 teaspoon vanilla
4 cups flour
4 ounces shredded coconut*
Powdered sugar

Cream butter, margarine, and sugar. Add vanilla and mix until fluffy. Add flour and coconut and mix well. Form dough into 3 long rolls and wrap individually in wax paper. Refrigerate for 8 hours or freeze for 2 hours.

Preheat oven to 300°F. Slice dough ¼-inch thick and bake on an ungreased cookie sheet for 25 to 30 minutes. Watch carefully and do not allow to brown. Cookies should be pale with just a hint of color. Cool on racks and sprinkle with powdered sugar.

Garden Café
Honolulu Academy of Arts
Honolulu, Hawai'i

O'ahu Ginger Snaps

Makes 4 dozen

½ cup butter
¼ cup vegetable shortening
1 cup sugar
¼ cup molasses
1 egg, beaten
2 cups flour
1 teaspoon ground ginger*
1 teaspoon ground cloves
1 teaspoon cinnamon
¼ teaspoon salt
2 teaspoons baking soda
Sugar

Preheat oven to 350°F. Cream butter, shortening, and sugar. Add molasses and egg. Beat well. Add sifted dry ingredients, mixing well. Chill dough and roll into small balls. Dip in sugar and bake for 10 minutes.

Note: Store in a tightly covered metal container to keep crisp.

Pecan Thins

Light and elegant dessert cookies.

1 cup unsalted butter, softened
¾ cup sugar
1 egg
1 teaspoon vanilla
1¾ cups unsifted flour
Pecan halves

Preheat oven to 350°F. Beat butter, eggs, sugar, and vanilla until light and fluffy. Add flour, beating until just combined. Drop dough by level teaspoonfuls, 2 inches apart, onto ungreased cookie sheets. Press pecan halves lightly down in the center of each cookie. Bake 8 to 10 minutes, or until edges of the cookies are golden brown. Let cool 1 minute, then transfer to wire racks to cool completely.

Coconut Macaroons

Makes about 1½ dozen

4 egg whites
¾ cup granulated sugar
½ teaspoon salt
1½ teaspoons vanilla extract
3 cups shredded coconut*
6 tablespoons all-purpose flour
8 ounces bittersweet chocolate

In a heavy saucepan stir together egg whites, sugar, salt, vanilla, and coconut. Sift in flour and stir until well-combined. Place over medium heat for 5 minutes, stirring constantly. Increase heat to medium-high and cook, stirring constantly, for 3 to 5 minutes until mixture has thickened and pulls away from side of the pan. Scrape mixture into a bowl and let cool slightly. Cover and chill just until cold.

Heat oven to 300°F. Lightly grease baking sheets. Using a small ice cream scoop, place dough 2 inches apart onto prepared baking sheets. Bake the macaroons in batches in the middle of oven for 20 to 25 minutes until pale golden. Remove from baking sheet and cool on wire rack.

Line a baking sheet or tray with foil. Finely chop chocolate. Place in a small metal bowl set over a pan of barely simmering water. Heat water to melt chocolate, stirring until smooth. Remove from heat and dip macaroon bottoms, one at a time, into chocolate, coating ¼-inch up the sides. Let any excess chocolate drip back into pan. Transfer coated macaroons to prepared tray and chill for 30 to 60 minutes until set. Store chilled and separated by layers of wax paper, in an airtight container.

Brownies
Hawaiian Style

Makes 4 dozen

4 ounces unsweetened chocolate
½ cup butter
4 eggs
1 cup sugar
2 teaspoons vanilla
1 cup flour
1 cup macadamia nuts,* chopped
1 (12-ounce) package semi-sweet chocolate chips
1 (7-ounce) package shredded coconut*

Preheat oven to 350°F. Melt chocolate and butter in heavy saucepan over low heat. Cool. Beat eggs until foamy. Gradually beat sugar and vanilla into eggs. Blend in chocolate mixture. Add flour and mix until combined. Stir in half of the macadamia nuts, chocolate chips, and coconut. Pour into a greased 9 x 13-inch baking pan and bake for 25 minutes or until brownies pull away from sides of pan.

Remove from oven and spread remaining macadamia nuts, chocolate chips, and coconut on top. Return to oven and bake for 10 more minutes. Cool. Cut into 1½-inch squares.

For healthier brownies from a packaged mix, substitute ½ cup non-fat or low-fat plain yogurt for oil and eggs.

Caramel Cuts

Makes 3 dozen

A favorite with generations of Punahou students.

½ cup melted butter
2 cups brown sugar
2 eggs
2 cups flour
2 teaspoons vanilla
2 teaspoons baking powder
¼ teaspoon salt
Chopped nuts (optional)

Preheat oven to 350°F. Combine butter and sugar. Add other ingredients and mix well. Bake in greased 15½ x 10½ x 1-inch pan for about 25 minutes. Cool and cut into bars.

Kalākaua Bars

Makes 2 dozen

Crust
1 cup flour
3 tablespoons powdered sugar
½ cup melted butter

Preheat oven to 350°F. Mix flour, powdered sugar, and butter. Press into an 8-inch square pan. Bake for 25 minutes.

Topping
2 eggs, slightly beaten
1 cup sugar
¼ cup flour
½ teaspoon baking powder
½ teaspoon salt
1 teaspoon vanilla
¾ cup chopped nuts
½ cup shredded coconut*
½ cup maraschino cherries

Mix ingredients together. Pour over crust and bake 25 minutes. Cool and slice.

Super Lemon Bars

Makes 2½ dozen

Crust
2 cups flour
½ cup macadamia nuts,* finely chopped
½ cup powdered sugar
1 cup butter

Preheat oven to 350°F. Combine flour, macadamia nuts, powdered sugar, and butter. Press into a greased 9 x 13-inch pan and bake for 20 to 25 minutes until golden brown.

Filling
¼ cup flour
½ teaspoon baking powder
4 eggs
2 cups sugar
½ cup lemon juice
1 teaspoon lemon zest (optional)
Powdered sugar

Combine flour, baking powder, eggs, sugar, lemon juice, and lemon zest. Mix well. Spread over baked crust. Bake until set, about 25 minutes. Cool. Dust top with sifted powdered sugar and cut into 3 x 1-inch bars.

Mauna Kea Bars

Makes 2 dozen

Crust
1¼ cups rolled oats
1¼ cups all-purpose flour
¾ cup shredded coconut*
¼ cup granulated sugar
½ teaspoon salt
¾ cup butter softened

Filling
¾ cup raspberry jam

Topping
3 egg whites
¼ teaspoon cream of tartar
⅔ cup granulated sugar

Heat oven to 325°F. In a large bowl, stir together oats, flour, coconut, sugar, and salt. Stir in butter, blending well. Press crust into bottom of a 9 x 13-inch baking pan. Bake 15 minutes until edges begin to brown. Let cool 5 minutes, spread evenly with jam, and set aside.

In a large bowl, whip egg whites and cream of tartar with an electric mixer on high speed until thick and foamy. Gradually add sugar and continue to whip until shiny and holds soft peaks.

Gently spread meringue evenly over jam using spatula. Bake about 20 minutes until meringue is lightly browned. Remove from oven and cool 5 minutes on wire rack. Cut into 24 bars and let cool completely before removing from pan with spatula.

Blueberry Bread Pudding   *Serves 8*

4 eggs
2 cups heavy or whipping cream
2 cups milk
1 cup packed light brown sugar
1 teaspoon vanilla extract
½ teaspoon ground cinnamon
6 cups cubed day-old bread
6 ounces white chocolate chips
2 cups fresh or 1 cup dried blueberries
3 tablespoons butter, melted

Amaretto Cream
¼ cup Amaretto
1 tablespoon cornstarch
1½ cups heavy cream
¼ cup granulated sugar

In a large bowl, beat eggs with a whisk until light and fluffy. Beat in cream, milk, brown sugar, vanilla, and cinnamon. Add bread, chocolate chips, and blueberries, stirring gently with spoon. Drizzle with melted butter and stir to mix. Let stand for 30 minutes for bread to absorb the egg mixture.

Heat oven to 350°F. Butter a 10 x 14-inch baking dish. Scrape in bread mixture, distributing evenly. Bake about 1 hour until firm when pressed in the center. Remove to wire rack and cool about 20 minutes until just warm.

In a small bowl, combine Amaretto and cornstarch with a whisk until smooth. In a medium saucepan, bring cream to a boil over medium heat. Add sugar and beat with a whisk until dissolved. Add Amaretto, stirring constantly with whisk and return to a boil. Reduce heat to low and cook, stirring until thickened.

Remove from heat and let cool to room temperature.

Top individual servings of bread pudding with Amaretto Cream.

Baked Coconut Custard with Lime Meringue

Serves 8

Coconut Custard
1 egg, beaten
4 egg yolks
½ teaspoon ground mace or nutmeg
½ cup granulated sugar
2½ cups shredded coconut
3 cups half-and-half
1 teaspoon vanilla extract

Lime Meringue
¼ teaspoon salt
4 egg whites
6 tablespoons sugar
½ teaspoon vanilla extract
1½ tablespoons fresh lime juice

Brandy Cream Sauce
½ cup heavy or whipping cream
¼ cup brandy

Butter eight 1½-inch deep individual baking dishes or ramekins. Arrange in large roasting pan and set aside. Heat over to 350°F.

In a large mixing bowl, beat together egg and egg yolks. Add mace and sugar, beating until light and fluffy. Stir in coconut, half-and-half, and vanilla. Fill prepared baking dishes ¾ full. Add enough boiling water to pan to fill 1-inch deep. Bake 35 to 40 minutes until firm.

Remove from oven and water baths. Reduce oven to 325°F. Top each dish with Lime Meringue, return to oven and bake 12 to 15 minutes until meringue is lightly golden. Remove to wire rack and cool. Serve at room temperature or chilled with a bit of Brandy Cream Sauce.

Lime Meringue: In a large bowl, add salt to egg whites. Beat with electric mixer until soft peaks form, about 4 minutes. Beat in sugar 1 tablespoon at a time. Continue beating to form stiff peaks. Beat in vanilla and lime juice. Cover and chill.

Brandy Cream Sauce: In a small bowl, whip cream until stiff. Fold in brandy. Cover and chill.

Apple Sweetbread Pudding

Serves 8 to 10

2 cups apples, peeled and thinly sliced
3 tablespoons plus ½ cup butter, divided
2 tablespoons lemon juice
½ cup brown sugar
2 tablespoons plus 1 teaspoon cinnamon, divided
1 (1-pound) loaf sweetbread
1 cup raisins
2 cups milk, scalded
1 cup sugar
5 eggs
1 teaspoon vanilla

Preheat oven to 350°F. Grease a 9 x 13-inch pan. Tear bread into 2-inch pieces and place in pan. In a medium saucepan, sauté apples in 3 tablespoons butter and lemon juice over medium-low heat. Add brown sugar and 2 tablespoons cinnamon and cook until sauce thickens. Remove from heat and set aside. Spread apple mixture over bread pieces. Sprinkle with raisins. Combine milk and ½ cup butter and stir until melted.

Stir in sugar. Beat eggs and vanilla in a separate bowl. Add eggs and remaining 1 teaspoon cinnamon to milk mixture and mix well. Pour over bread. Bake for 30 minutes. Serve warm or chilled.

Michel's Grand Marnier Soufflé

Serves 8

¼ pound unsalted butter
2½ cups flour
3¼ cups milk, warmed
8 egg yolks
4 whole eggs
1 cup Grand Marnier
4 egg whites
½ cup sugar
Powdered sugar

Preheat oven to 375°F. Heat the butter in a saucepan over moderate heat. Add the flour and stir until well-blended. Add the warm milk and stir until very thick, making sure the mixture does not stick to the edge of the pan. Remove from heat, and beating constantly, add the egg yolks one-by-one. Continue beating while adding the whole eggs. Stir in the Grand Marnier. Beat egg whites until stiff. Continue beating while adding the sugar. Fold into the flour-egg mixture gently. Gently fold meringue into egg mixture.

Butter individual soufflé dishes with unsalted butter and dust with flour. Fill dishes ¾ full with batter and bake for 18 minutes. Remove from oven, dust with powdered sugar, and serve immediately.

Michel's at the Colony Surf
Honolulu, Hawai'i

Quick Cool Lemon Soufflé

2 envelopes unflavored gelatin
½ cup water
6 eggs
1½ cups sugar
1½ cups heavy cream
1 tablespoon grated lemon peel
⅔ cup lemon juice
Garnish: mint leaves

Prepare collar on a 1-quart soufflé dish. In a small saucepan, sprinkle gelatin over water and let soften for 10 minutes. Cook over low heat until gelatin dissolves. Cool.

Combine eggs and sugar in a large bowl and beat at high speed until light. Whip cream and refrigerate.

Combine grated lemon peel and juice with cooled gelatin and blend into egg-sugar mixture. Chill until mixture is thick enough to mound. Fold in whipped cream. Pour into soufflé dish and refrigerate 3 hours. Remove collar, garnish, and serve.

Chocolate Mousse

Serves 4

1 envelope unflavored gelatin
¼ cup water
4 ounces semi-sweet chocolate
2 ounces unsweetened chocolate
1¼ cups heavy whipping cream
¼ cup sugar
Garnish: chocolate shavings

In a small saucepan, sprinkle gelatin over water and let soften for 3 minutes. Cook over low heat until gelatin dissolves. Bring mixture to a simmer and add sugar stirring until dissolved. Do not boil. Set aside.

Melt chocolate in a double boiler. Transfer the melted chocolate to a separate bowl. Gradually add gelatin mixture to chocolate, whisking with each addition. Whip cream and sugar into soft peaks. Set aside enough to garnish top of mousse. Stir half of the whipped cream into chocolate mixture to lighten. Then take chocolate mixture and, while electric mixer is on low, pour into remaining whipped cream. Blend on low to incorporate chocolate. Increase speed to high and whip for a total of 10 to 15 seconds. Spoon into parfait or champagne glasses and chill for 1 to 2 hours or until firm. Garnish with reserved whipped cream and chocolate shavings.

To make chocolate shavings, run a vegetable peeler down the side of a slightly warmed chocolate bar.

Coconut Mousse

Heavenly!

> 1 pint half-and-half
> 3 envelopes unflavored gelatin
> ⅓ cup water
> 1 cup sugar
> 2 cups grated coconut*
> 1½ pints whipping cream
> 1 teaspoon coconut extract

In a saucepan, bring half-and-half to a boil. Dissolve gelatin in water. Add gelatin mixture and sugar, cooking until sugar dissolves. Cool and add coconut. Beat coconut extract and cream until stiff. Fold in whipped cream and pour into an 8-cup mold. Chill until firm.

Coconut Pearl
Tapioca Pudding

Serves 6

5 cups milk
½ cup granulated sugar
¾ cup small pearl tapioca
12 to 14 ounces canned coconut milk*
1 cup frozen passion fruit* juice concentrate, thawed
1 to 2 teaspoons fresh lemon juice

In a large saucepan, combine milk and sugar and cook over medium heat until simmering, stirring frequently. Add tapioca, reduce heat to low, and simmer, stirring frequently for 45 to 60 minutes until tapioca pearls are soft. Stir in coconut milk and cook 15 minutes more, stirring frequently.

Pour into individual serving bowls. Let cool, cover, and chill overnight. In a small bowl or pitcher with spout, stir together passion fruit concentrate and lemon juice. Cover and chill. Serve puddings topped with passion fruit syrup.

Bambi's Flan

½ cup sugar

Melt sugar in a saucepan over low heat until golden in color. Quickly pour into 8-inch round metal cake pan. Set aside.

Note: Sugar will harden immediately.

8 eggs, separated
1 cup sugar
3 cups warm milk
1 teaspoon vanilla
½ teaspoon salt

Preheat oven to 350°F. Beat egg yolks in a large bowl until light in color. Slowly beat in sugar. Continue beating while gradually adding milk, vanilla, salt, and egg whites. In order to remove all air bubbles, pour mixture through a fine strainer into the pan of hardened sugar. Set pan into a larger pan containing 1 inch of water. Bake for 1 hour or until knife comes out clean. Chill. Loosen sides and turn upside down onto a platter.

Pineapple with Liliko'i Cream

1 fresh pineapple*
12 ounces cream cheese, softened
6 ounces liliko'i juice concentrate
¾ cup finely diced ripe mango*
4 ounces strawberries, diced
2 tablespoons granulated sugar

Twist off top and peel pineapple. Cut in half crosswise. Stand one half of pineapple upright. Position a large sharp knife at top of pineapple, and cut downward to slice pineapple into eight pieces. Set aside two center pieces containing core. Repeat with the other half of pineapple. Remove flesh from core sections and save for another use. Discard core. Beat together cream cheese and liliko'i juice concentrate in a food processor or electric mixer until very smooth. Scrape into a bowl. Fold mango into cream cheese mixture and refrigerate for at least 2 hours until firm. Place strawberries and sugar in a food processor or blender and purée until smooth. Cover and refrigerate.

Heat broiler. Grease a baking sheet. Lay pineapple slices on baking sheet. Broil until lightly browned, 5 to 10 minutes.

Lay one slice of broiled pineapple on each of four plates. Spread with liliko'i cream, top with another slice of pineapple and more liliko'i cream. Finish with a third slice of pineapple. Drizzle with strawberry sauce. Serve.

Note: Guanabana, also called soursop, is a white-fleshed fruit popular in Latino cooking. The purée is sold frozen and can be used in place of the liliko'i.

Chocolate Truffles *Makes about 2 dozen*

¾ cup heavy cream
4 tablespoons unsalted butter, cut into small pieces
10 ounces bittersweet chocolate, chopped
1 tablespoon brandy
2 teaspoons grated lime zest
2 teaspoons minced crystallized ginger*
Unsweetened cocoa powder or finely shredded coconut*

Place cream and butter in a saucepan. Bring to a full boil over medium heat, stirring frequently. Turn off heat. Add chocolate bits. Gently stir to melt chocolate. Let stand 5 minutes. Add brandy, lime zest, and ginger, whisking slowly to combine. Scrape mixture into a bowl using a rubber spatula. Cover and refrigerate until firm, about 4 hours or overnight.

Line a baking sheet with waxed or parchment paper. Using a melon baller or very small ice cream scoop, portion chocolate and roll between palms of hands to form mixture into 1-inch balls. If mixture is too hard, let stand at room temperature 5 to 10 minutes before shaping. Place on prepared pan. Chill 10 to 15 minutes to firm.

Place a small amount of cocoa in a small deep dish. Remove chocolate balls from refrigerator. Roll each ball between the palms of hands to warm up slightly. Drop in cocoa and swirl to coat. Return truffles to baking sheet. Chill at least 1 hour until firm. Store in airtight container in refrigerator.

Crunchy Baked Mangoes   *Serves 4 to 6*

Island version of apple crisp.

4 medium mangoes,* peeled and thinly sliced
½ cup sugar
¾ cup quick-cooking rolled oats
¾ cup brown sugar
½ cup flour
1 teaspoon cinnamon
½ cup butter or margarine

Preheat oven to 350°F. Toss mangoes with sugar. Place in a greased 8-inch round pan. Combine oats, brown sugar, flour, and cinnamon. Cut in butter until mixture is crumbly. Sprinkle evenly over mangoes. Bake for 35 to 40 minutes or until top crust is browned and crisp. Serve warm with ice cream.

Note: Ripeness of mangoes will determine the amount of sugar needed. Use less sugar with riper mangoes.

Undoubtedly the most popular fruit tree in the state, the first mango trees were introduced to Hawai'i from Manila in 1824 by Captain John Meek of the Kamehameha. Indigenous to Southern Asia, the mango has made its way to many subtropical regions of the world. It is a medium-sized fruit, with patches of crimson, purple, green, and golden yellow when ripe. The most common of mangoes, Hayden, comes from Florida, while the Pirie has its origins in India. There are many varieties of mangoes, but the better ones are chosen for their sweet flavor, smooth texture, and juiciness. It is an excellent source of vitamin A, and when half-ripe or green, a good source of vitamin C. Mango season runs throughout the summer. It is eaten fresh as a dessert fruit, used for sauces, in salads or in desserts. Green, it can be made into chutney, pickled or dried and preserved as mango seed.

Macadamia Popcorn Crunch

Makes 8 cups

7 cups popped popcorn
1 (5-ounce) can macadamia nuts* coarsely chopped
¾ cup brown sugar
⅓ cup margarine
3 tablespoons light corn syrup
¼ teaspoon vanilla
¼ teaspoon baking soda

Preheat oven to 300°F. Combine popcorn and macadamia nuts in a large, greased saucepan and place in oven while syrup is cooking. Combine brown sugar, margarine, and corn syrup in a heavy saucepan over medium heat. Bring to a boil, stirring constantly with a wooden spoon. Boil for 4 minutes, stirring occasionally. The mixture should boil at a moderate rate over entire surface. Remove from heat. Stir in baking soda and vanilla. Pour over macadamia nuts and popcorn and stir until well-coated. Bake for 10 minutes. Remove from oven and stir. Return to oven for another 5 minutes. Spread mixture onto aluminum foil to cool. Cool completely, then break up. Store in an airtight container.

Macadamia nuts were first brought to Hawai'i by William Purvis in 1882. The trees are medium sized with shiny, holly-like leaves. The white nuts are enclosed in a brittle shell which in turn is covered by a husk. The nuts fall to the ground when mature where they are gathered, de-husked, dried, and upon roasting, cracked open. Macadamia nuts are harvested from August to January. The peak season is October through November. Although some of the other islands have joined in the production of macadamia nuts, the Island of Hawai'i is still the largest commercial producer.

Goody Goody
Serves 8 to 10

A Maui favorite on hot sunny days.

3 (12-ounce) cans strawberry soda
1 (14-ounce) can sweetened condensed milk

Mix strawberry soda and sweetened condensed milk and pour into a metal baking dish. Freeze until partially frozen, about 1 to 2 hours. Beat the mixture, then return to freezer and freeze completely.

This cool, sherbet-like treat, originally named Guri Guri* is sold at Maui Mall and at a stand near the old stadium park here in Honolulu.

Papaya Sorbet
Serves 8 to 10

3 large papayas,* peeled, seeded and pureed (about 2½ cups)
¼ cup lemon juice
1 envelope unflavored gelatin
½ cup orange juice
¾ cup sugar
¼ cup honey
1 cup whipping cream

Combine papaya purée and lemon juice. Soften gelatin in orange juice, then dissolve over boiling water. Blend sugar and honey with whipping cream. Gradually stir in gelatin and papaya purée. Pour into ice trays and freeze for 1 hour or until half-frozen. Beat the mixture, then return to freezer and freeze completely.

Macadamia Nut Parfait Sauce

Makes 2 cups

Great over ice cream. Makes a lovely holiday gift.

⅓ cup water
⅓ cup brown sugar
1 cup light corn syrup
1 cup macadamia nut bits* or chopped pecans

Bring water to a boil. Add sugar and dissolve. Add corn syrup and return mixture to a boil. Place nuts in a jar and pour in sugar mixture. Refrigerate until ready to serve. Sauce will thicken as it cools.

Note: Sauce keeps well in the refrigerator.

Pineapple Brandy Sauce

Makes 1 cup

1 (8-ounce) can crushed pineapple,* drained
1 tablespoon brandy
2 tablespoons brown sugar

Heat ingredients and serve with Two Crust Banana Pie (see page 233) or vanilla ice cream.

Brandied Hard Sauce

Makes 1½ cups

⅓ cup butter, softened
1 cup powdered sugar
Pinch salt
2 tablespoons brandy

Combine ingredients, mixing well until creamy and smooth.

Grand Marnier Sauce

Makes 1½ cups

1 cup whipping cream
½ cup sugar
3 teaspoons lemon juice
7 tablespoons Grand Marnier
1½ teaspoons grated orange peel

In a medium bowl, whip cream until soft peaks are formed.
Fold in sugar, lemon juice, Grand Marnier, and orange peel.
Refrigerate. Serve with Grand Marnier Soufflé or fresh fruit.

Hawaiian Fish and Seafood Chart

by Margo Stahl, Marine Biologist

Fish have long been recognized as having unique nutritional as well as a cosmopolitan gustatory appeal. Although some oily fish suffer from the stigma of being "fishy," most fish contain less than five percent fat. This fat has remarkable food value. Not only do fish contain high proportions of polyunsaturated fatty acids, they also contain relatively small amounts of cholesterol. Consequently, fish and shellfish are frequently recommended for those individuals seeking more healthful diets.

Hawai'i has many delectable species of fish and shellfish. This chart will introduce you to some of the local favorites.

Tunas

Tunas are commercially the most important group of fishes in Hawai'i. Their silvery bodies can range in size up to several hundred pounds. They are marked with dark areas on top and light undersides; this countershading allows them to blend in with their environment. Good table quality tuna flesh has a translucent rosy to red color. The older and bigger the fish, the deeper the hue of the flesh. They are usually bought in fillets. Sashimi, raw tuna, is an Island delicacy. Cooking tends to make the taste and smell of tuna more pronounced.

Aku, Skipjack Tuna, Ocean Bonito, Katsuo

Aku is canned for export. When eaten raw, as sashimi, it has a surprisingly delicate flavor. Try baking a whole small aku, basted in soy sauce and liquid smoke and wrapped in foil.

'Ahi, Yellowfin Tuna, Shibi

'Ahi flesh is lighter in color than aku. Raw 'ahi is an excellent choice for sashimi or it may be sautéed in sesame oil with soy sauce, chili peppers, and green onions.

Ahipalaha, Albacore, Tonbo

Albacore tuna have the whitest flesh of any of the tunas and frequently command a high price. Peak landings are in the summer and most fish are very large.

Billfish

A'u, Pacific Blue Marlin, Kajiki

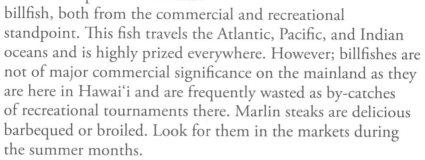

The blue marlin is presently the most important Hawaiian billfish, both from the commercial and recreational standpoint. This fish travels the Atlantic, Pacific, and Indian oceans and is highly prized everywhere. However; billfishes are not of major commercial significance on the mainland as they are here in Hawai'i and are frequently wasted as by-catches of recreational tournaments there. Marlin steaks are delicious barbequed or broiled. Look for them in the markets during the summer months.

A'u, Striped Marlin, Naraigi

This species is the next most
important billfish in the
Hawaiian markets and is found
throughout the Indo-Pacific region. It is similar to
the blue marlin and can be found as steaks or fillets alongside
blue marlin during the summer months.

A'u, Broadbill Swordfish

Found throughout the world,
the controversial federal ban
on swordfish reported to contain
high levels of mercury has done little to
discourage its popularity and high market prices. It is usually
sold in fresh or frozen inch-thick steaks during the summer
and fall months. The meat is firm and of distinctive flavor. It
is best either oven broiled or charcoaled.

Snappers

*There are many taste-tempting snappers found in Hawaiian
waters. The Penguin Bank-North Moloka'i region and the remote
Northwestern Hawaiian Islands are prime fishing grounds.
Snappers are usually brightly colored with red and yellow hues.
The flesh of the snapper is white, firm yet tender, characteristically
mild, and tasteful. The holiday season brings the greatest demand,
accompanied by higher prices.*

'Ōpakapaka

An Island favorite, this pink
snapper is usually available
from two to twelve pounds. It is
delicious baked, fried, broiled, or as
sashimi. Catches of 'ōpakapaka are greatest in December.

Kalekale

This pinkish fish is a prized addition to any table. It can frequently be purchased from 1 to 4 pounds.

Onaga

This beautiful red fish is ranked near the top for taste among the snappers. Locally, this red snapper can reach a size of 36 pounds, but more often, it will range from 1 to 15 pounds. It is available in the markets particularly around New Year's.

Ehu

This large-eyed fish may weigh up to 12 pounds, but it is commonly purchased between 1 and 5 pounds. Like its relative, the onaga, it is caught at depths of 600 to 1,000 feet. Ehu is available year-round, with greatest supplies in December.

Uku

This gray snapper has mean-looking canine teeth and averages 7 to 8 pounds. It can reach up to 50 pounds, however. Unlike the other snappers, it is more available in the summer.

Taape

This snapper is yellow. Recently, young taape were deliberately introduced into our waters. The introduction was quite successful and now they are very abundant in the market at reasonable prices year-round. Size ranges from ½ to 1 pound, making them an ideal size for pan frying.

Grouper

Hāpuʻupuʻu
This is the only grouper of any major commercial significance in Hawaiʻi. It is a white, firm-fleshed fish, ranging in size up to 50 pounds. Delicious baked or cubed and stir-fried with vegetables. Maximum landings of this fish are in September, but it can be purchased year-round.

Jacks

Ulua, Pāpio
Ulua refers to any one of eleven different species of large Jacks. The white ulua is slightly higher priced than the black. They all have a firm, white flakey flesh. The silver ulua and pig ulua are also delicious. Pāpio are the young of the several species of ulua and refer to ulua under 10 pounds. They are delicious pan-fried. The head is excellent as the basis for fish chowder. Available most of the year.

Akule, Hahalalū, Pāʻāʻā, Big-Eyed Scad, Aji

This large eyed, mackerel-looking fish is oilier with more dark muscle area. The dark muscle is more flavorful, like light and dark meat in chicken. The fish is moist with a coarse texture. Try them fried, baked, smoked, or dried. They are especially available from February through August.

'Ōpelu, Mackerel Scad
This fish is similar to akule. It is considered "fishy" by some. It is delicious dried and smoked. Look for this fish in the fall.

High Seas Fish

Mahimahi, Dolphinfish, Mansaku
A large fish with delicate firm white flesh. It is available fresh in fish markets, though most of our frozen mahimahi is imported. The price varies greatly between fresh and frozen fish. Mahimahi is frequently featured in local restaurants. It is especially popular fried in egg batter. The dolphinfish is not to be confused with the porpoise. It is available here year-round. It can also be found on the East and West coasts although it is not as popular.

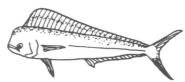

Ono, Wahoo, Sawara
Ono has a very moist, slightly coarse white flesh (not quite as firm as mahimahi). The fish averages 40 to 100 pounds, therefore it is usually purchased as ono steaks rather than whole. Excellent broiled or sautéed. Available year-round.

Nearshore Fish

Kūmū, Goatfish
This fish is red in color and has firm white flesh. It can reach six to nine pounds, however, it is frequently available in smaller sizes, from ½ to 3½ pounds. Steamed Kūmū is an Island specialty. Available year-round.

Mullet

There are several species of mullet in Hawaiian waters, although most restaurants import it for their menu. Island-raised pond mullet are also available. The average weight is 1½ pounds. For a taste treat steam mullet with ginger and green onions. It is obtainable year-round.

Shellfish

Lobster

Local lobster tails come from the Northwestern Hawaiian Islands. Depending on the weather, they are available year-round.

Shrimp

We are fortunate to have delicious marine shrimp, some of which are caught in very deep water. This expanding fishery is providing fresh and frozen shrimp to numerous local restaurants. As this fishery is developed, availability will increase.

Hawaiian Freshwater Prawn

Freshwater prawns are an important part of Hawai'i's expanding aquaculture industry. These delicately flavored prawns taste great in garlic butter and ginger. Available year-round.

Glossary

'Ahi—One of the most popular fish in Hawai'i. The name 'ahi applies to all the larger varieties of tuna found in Hawaiian waters, such as albacore, yellowfin, and big-eye tuna. Raw 'ahi is often used for sashimi. 'Ahi is most abundant from late spring through September.

Aku—Aku refers to the Skipjack Tuna and the Ocean Bonito. Aku is usually canned for export. When eaten raw, as sashimi, it has a surprisingly delicate flavor.

A'u—A'u is the Hawaiian name for marlin. This large billfish is tasty and lean. It is most abundant during the summer. A'u can be poached, fried, or marinated and then broiled. A'u may be substituted with shark or swordfish in most recipes.

Baby Corn—This is a tiny new ear of corn which comes canned.

Balsamic Vinegar—This dark brown vinegar comes from Modena, Italy. It requires six or more years to be processed and has a sweet-tart flavor.

Bamboo Shoots—Bamboo shoots or takenoko have a hearty, firm texture suitable for simmered dishes and one-pot cookery. The canned variety is widely used.

Bean Sprouts—Sprouted mung beans are available in markets and health food stores. Bean sprouts may be purchased fresh or canned.

Black Beans—Chinese black beans are cooked, salted, and fermented soy beans. To prepare, rinse beans and then mash them with the back of a spoon.

Breadfruit—Large melon-size starchy fruit that can be eaten either half ripe or very ripe. The ripe stage should be baked and flavored like a yam or sliced thinly and deep-fried. The half ripe stage is peeled and steamed or boiled. Can be used instead of potatoes in a stew.

Butterfish—Black cod, a high fat, strongly flavored fish used in Japanese cuisine. May substitute bluefish, sheepshead, or other oily fish.

Capers—The flower buds of the caper plant. This condiment is salted and preserved in vinegar.

Char Siu—Marinated pork that is reddish pink in color and has a sweet spicy flavor. The meat is usually roasted or barbecued. Char siu is often added to stir-fry dishes.

Chicken Lū'au—Chicken cooked with coconut milk and taro or spinach leaves.

Chili Oil—Oil flavored with hot chilies. It is used as a seasoning in many Chinese dishes. It has a shelf life of approximately six months. Keeps its flavor longer if refrigerated.

Chinese Five Spice—This unusual seasoning contains star anise, anise pepper, fennel, cloves, and cinnamon in varying quantities. The Chinese name is Ng Heong Fun.

Chinese Parsley—A coriander spice plant which is also known as cilantro. The strong flavor of the leaves is important in Chinese and other Asian cooking.

Chutney—A spicy condiment made with fruits, spices, sugar, and vinegar. An accompaniment to meats and curried foods.

Cilantro—(See Chinese Parsley)

Cloud Ears—A dried fungus with no real flavor of its own. The somewhat crunchy consistency and the dark color add interest to a variety of Asian dishes. When soaked in water, it expands to five times its size.

Coconut—The nut or fruit of a coconut palm tree. The creamy, white meat of the young coconut fruit can be easily removed with a spoon. The meat of the mature coconut is firm and is usually grated. Shredded and flaked coconut is available in cans or packages.

Coconut Milk—Coconut milk is made by simmering water and fresh coconut pulp. The mixture is then strained through a cheesecloth. Coconut milk is available frozen.

Coconut Syrup—Coconut syrup is made from coconut water, grated fresh coconut, sugar, and cream of tartar.

Coconut Water—The liquid found in the center of a coconut. There are three eyes on the top of the coconut which can be opened to drain the liquid.

Cuttlefish—Similar to squid (calamari). Available fresh, frozen, and dried.

Da Kine—Catch-all phrase for miscellaneous items.

Daikon—A common ingredient in Japanese cooking. It is in the turnip family though it is more radish-like in flavor. Any turnip may be used as a substitute.

Dijon Mustard—This condiment originated in Dijon, France. It is a combination of dry mustard, herbs, spices, and white wine. Dijon mustard goes well with meats, fish, and poultry.

Dim Sum—Dim Sum are Chinese dumplings with wheat flour or glutenous rice dough wrappings that are filled with flavorful mixtures of pork, beef, fish, or vegetables. Dim sum are steamed, baked, or fried.

Dried Red Curry Stock—A powder made from dried red chili, spices, coconut cream, and salt. Identified with Thai cooking.

Feta Cheese—This cheese is made from ewe's milk or ewe's and goat's milk. It is a soft cheese with a sharp and salty flavor which may be used in cooking.

Fish Cake—Also known as Kamaboko, this is a puréed steamed loaf of whitefish. The outer surface is sometimes tinted bright pink. Can be deep-fried, broiled, or steamed.

Fish Sauce—An anchovy-based, dark sauce with a strong aroma used to flavor Southeast Asian food. Fish sauce is rich in B vitamins and protein.

Fontina Cheese—A semi-soft to hard cheese made with cow's milk. It has a light yellow color and a delicate nutty flavor.

Furikake—Seasoning for rice and noodles containing seaweed, sesame seeds, and salt. Adds color and flavor.

Ginger—A gnarled light brown root with a pungent, spicy flavor. Garlic and ginger are the basic flavors in many stir-fry dishes. Peel and slice, mince or grate for maximum flavor. The Japanese use a special ginger grater with fine teeth to make a fresh paste. Ginger juice may be obtained by squeezing a small chunk of ginger in a garlic press. To store, refrigerate in a jar of sherry or freeze in a plastic bag.

Ginger Slivers—(See Ginger)

Guava—Tropical fruit the size of an apricot or plum with a unique flavor. The entire cavity of the fruit is comprised of seed. It is used primarily in juice, preserves, jellies, sauces, and syrups or eaten raw. It is readily available in Hawai'i, California, and Florida. Canned guava shells can be purchased in the gourmet section of markets or specialty shops.

Hana Ebi—Dried shredded shrimp. Available in green and red, it is used for color as well as flavor. Available in the Oriental section of most markets.

Hana Katsuo—Dried shaved bonito flakes that resemble rose colored wood shavings. Sold in cellophane packages.

Haupia—Coconut pudding eaten as a dessert.

Hawaiian Chili Pepper—A small, attractive orange red fruit used as a spicy seasoning.

Hawaiian Rock Salt—Salt used for cooking. It is available in white and red, which has been colored with clay. Coarse salt or kosher salt can be substituted.

Hoisin Sauce—Fermented bean sauce that is sweet and pungent. Made from soy beans with garlic, glutenous red rice, salt, and sugar. It is used as a condiment with dishes such as pork or roast duck and is often an ingredient in a marinade for poultry.

Hot Pepper Sauce—A watery, orange-red, bottled sauce that is used to add spicy hot seasoning to chili, seafood, and sauces.

'Inamona—Kukui nut paste used for flavoring in poke or as a condiment for other lū'au dishes.

Japanese Cucumber—This slender elongated cucumber is crunchy and flavorful. It retains these qualities when combined with other ingredients better than the Western cucumber. The skin does not need to be peeled.

Jicama—A brownish-gray skinned root vegetable resembling a turnip with crisp white sweet meat. It is sliced and eaten raw in salads or as a crudité, or cooked in stews. Lemon juice will keep raw jicama from turning brown. Jicama is sometimes called Chinese yam or Chop-suey yam.

Kalbi—Beef short ribs marinated in a Korean sauce with a soy sauce and sesame base.

Kamaboko—(See Fish Cake)

Kampyo—Dried gourd strips used in Asian cooking. Kampyo needs to be soaked or cooked before using. It is often found in Japanese sushi. Also spelled kanpyo.

Ketjap Manis—A Javanese sauce made with soy sauce, palm syrup, garlic, star anise, salam leaves (a tropical laurel-like tree), and galangal (a relative of ginger). Ketjap manis is a fundamental ingredient in Javanese cooking.

Kim Chee—Korean pickled cabbage served as a relish. Includes onions, radishes, garlic, and chilies. Sold in refrigerated section of grocery stores.

Kona Coffee—Kona coffee is medium bodied, richly flavored, and aromatic. It is grown on the southwest coast of the Big Island of Hawai'i.

Kwo Pee—Dried orange peel. Also spelled gwoh pay.

Laulau—Steamed bundle of pork, fish, and beef. Wrapped in taro or spinach leaves and enclosed in ti leaves.

Lemon Grass—The fragrant gray-green lemon grass grows two feet long on a small bulbous base. The bottom six to eight inches of the stalk is used for cooking after the tough outer leaves are removed.

Li Hing Mui—Preserved plum with or without the seed. It has a sweet, salty, licorice flavor.

Limu Kohu—A soft, succulent, small red seaweed used in raw fish dishes.

Lomi Lomi Salmon—A chilled fish dish of salted salmon, onions, green onions, and tomatoes. Traditionally served at lūʻau.

Long Rice—Dried bean curd thread-like noodles. Made from mung bean flour. Must be soaked in water before cooking to absorb flavor of food with which they are cooked.

Lumpia—A Filipino appetizer similar to a spring roll.

Lumpia Wrapper—A rectangular shaped pastry used to wrap around a meat filling. Size and shape distinguish it from a won ton pi.

Lup Cheong Sausage—Chinese sausage flavored with anise. It is slightly sweet with a licorice flavor and very fatty.

Lychee—A traditional Chinese fruit with a woody exterior around a sweet fleshy white flavored pulp. Fresh lychee may be frozen. Canned lychee is peeled and often seeded.

Macadamia Nuts—A member of the protea family, this nut is a delicacy. Can be purchased whole, in pieces or in bits. For cooking, unsalted nuts are preferred. Macadamia nuts freeze very well.

Mahimahi—(See fish chart)

Malasada—Portuguese doughnut.

Mandarin Orange—A small yellow to red-orange citrus fruit whose family includes the tangerine, temple orange, and Japanese satsuma orange. Canned mandarin oranges are the Satsuma variety from Japan.

Mango—A tropical yellow pink fruit with bright orange flesh. Has a high fiber content. Best known varieties are Haden, Pirie, and

Gouveia. A ripe mango is slightly soft and has a strong fragrance.

Mānoa Lettuce—A leafy, semi-head lettuce also known as Green Mignonette, named after a verdant valley on the island of Oʻahu. Any leafy green lettuce may be substituted.

Maui Onion—A sweet and mild onion. It is a Texas Bermuda Granex Grano type onion grown in volcanic soil. A Texas onion or a Vidalia sweet onion can be substituted.

Mirin—Heavily sweetened rice wine used for flavoring or in marinades, it is an important ingredient in Japanese cooking. One teaspoon of sugar may be substituted for one tablespoon of mirin.

Miso—A fermented soy paste used in soups and stews. Aka miso is a dark red strongly flavored miso and shiro miso is a white, sweet, mildly flavored miso.

Mullet—(See fish chart)

Nairagi—This striped marlin is an important billfish in the Hawaiian market and is found throughout the Indo-Pacific region. It is similar to the blue marlin and can be found as steaks or fillets at the fish market during the summer months.

Nori—Thin sheets of dark green or purplish dry seaweed used to wrap sushi or mochi (rice balls), adding color and a distinctive taste to the rice. Most commonly available in cellophane packages, usually ten sheets to a package. It may also be available in canisters or tin boxes.

Ogo—Ogo is a common name for limu manaea, a species of Hawaiian seaweed.

Olive Oil—A flavorful oil used in many Italian dishes. Extra virgin olive oil is obtained from the first pressing of the olives and is recommended for its light, delicate flavor.

Onaga—This beautiful red fish is ranked near the top for taste among the snappers. Locally this red snapper can reach a size of thirty-six pounds, but more often it will range from one to fifteen pounds. It is available in the markets particularly around the New Year.

Opal Basil—A type of basil with crinkled purple leaves and pale pink flowers.

Oyster Sauce—Spiced concentrated liquid in which oysters have been cooked.

Papaya—A pear or light-bulb-shaped yellow fruit with melon-like flesh. A ripe papaya has yellow skin with an occasional patch of green. It should be firm to touch. The skin is not eaten.

Papaya Seeds—These peppercorn-sized black seeds are found in the center of fresh papayas. To use papaya seeds in cooking, scoop out and rinse. Remove all the papaya flesh and fibers. Dry well. Ground papaya seeds impart a peppery flavor and are often used in salad dressings.

Parmesan Cheese—A hard cheese made from partly skimmed milk. The flavor intensifies with age. Whenever possible, use freshly grated Parmesan cheese.

Passion Fruit—A plum-size fruit with a tangy citrus-like taste. Juice is extracted and used as a flavoring. It is available as a frozen concentrate. Also called liliko‘i.

Peanut Oil—A favorite oil in Chinese cooking, peanut oil can tolerate high temperatures without smoking. It is not likely to burn. Because it has a high smoke point, it does not pick up odors and flavors and may be strained and used again.

Pepperoncini—These mild, light green peppers are long and cone shaped. They are an essential ingredient in Italian antipasto. Pepperoncini is sometimes labeled as Greek peppers or sweet Italian peppers. It is also spelled pepperocini.

Pickled Ginger—Baby ginger that has been pickled in sweet vinegar and then either slivered or sliced. It is used as a garnish or palate refresher. It comes in red or pink.

Pickled Scallions—Otherwise known as rankyo or rakkyo, this Japanese condiment can be found in cans.

Pineapple—The pineapple is a pine cone-shaped fruit with a horny rind that grows on a low cactus-like plant. Each plant produces one fruit every twenty to twenty-four months. The pineapple is native to South America.

Pipikaula—Hawaiian beef jerky. It is cured dried beef.

Poi—Steamed taro root pounded into a thick paste.

Poke—Fresh raw fish mixed with seaweed, kukui nut paste, hot red peppers, sesame seeds, or any other combination to make a fish salad.

Portuguese Sausage—Highly seasoned pork sausage. Red pepper is liberally used in this sausage. It is available mild or hot. Spicy Italian sausage may be substituted.

Pūpū—Finger food. Literally, a relish, snack, or hors d'oeuvre.

Rice Flour—Made from steamed glutenous rice. Used for dumplings and confections, as well as a thickener for sauces.

Rice Vinegar—Vinegar made from fermented rice. It is lighter and sweeter than most Western vinegars. It is also called Japanese rice vinegar or Tamanoe vinegar.

Rice Wine—A Japanese wine known as sake, which is used in cooking and as a beverage. Dry sherry may be substituted.

Romano Cheese—A hard cheese made from cow's milk and aged for eight to twelve months. It has a salty, sharp taste and is grated for use in most recipes. Pecorino romano cheese is made with sheep's milk.

Sesame Oil—Oil pressed from the sesame seed. Highly concentrated and very flavorful. It is especially prevalent in Korean and Chinese cooking.

Sesame Seeds—Aromatic white or black seeds often used in Asian cooking. May be purchased plain or roasted.

Shiitake Mushrooms—Shiitake mushrooms have brown or black caps from one to three inches in diameter Although fresh shiitake mushrooms are available, the thick, dried mushrooms are far superior.

Snow Peas—Also known as Chinese peas or sugar peas, snow peas are light green and crisp. The entire pod is edible and may be found frozen or fresh. To prepare, remove strings.

Somen Noodles—Thin fine round white Japanese noodles that cook quickly. They are shorter and thinner than spaghetti noodles.

Soy Sauce—A liquid made of soy beans, barley, and salt used as the principal seasoning in Oriental cooking. Also known as shoyu.

Squid Lūʻau—Squid cooked with coconut milk and taro or spinach leaves.

Star Anise—A star-shaped dried spice with a delicate licorice flavor.

Steam or Steaming—Steaming in a bowl can be accomplished by placing an empty tuna can, with the top and bottom removed, in a Dutch oven filled with two inches of water. Place bowl on top. Cover and steam.

Taro Leaves—Also called lūʻau leaves, they are similar to spinach leaves in texture and taste.

Tarragon Vinegar—A vinegar, usually white wine vinegar flavored with fresh tarragon.

Teriyaki—Barbecued or broiled beef or poultry marinated in soy sauce, flavored with ginger, garlic, and brown sugar.

Thai Fish Sauce—An anchovy based, dark sauce used to flavor Thai food. Oriental food stores usually carry this.

Ti Leaves—Large smooth green leaves of the ti plant. The leaves are used as "wrappers" for a variety of island dishes.

Tofu—Bean curd or cake, it is white with a custard-like consistency. Usually comes in blocks packed in water.

Ume Boshi—Unripe plums soaked in brine and packed with red shiso leaves, which flavor and dye the plums pinkish-red.

Wasabi—A hot green horseradish powder used in Japanese cooking. Mix powder with water to form a smooth paste. It may also be called Japanese Green Horseradish. Do not substitute regular horseradish. Wasabi has a very long shelf life.

Water Chestnuts—Crispy, white vegetables covered with a thin, fine, brown-black skin. If fresh, pare before using. If available, they are well worth the effort. Canned, they are readily available.

Watercress—A green leafy plant that grows in shallow fresh running water. The leaves have a peppery flavor. Watercress is usually blanched or stir-fried. The leaves and tender stems are used and the tough stems are discarded.

Wine Vinegar—This vinegar is made by fermenting white, red, or rose wine. The type of wine will determine the flavor and color of the vinegar.

Wok—Chinese frying pan specifically designed for stir-frying. The shape provides for intense heat at the bottom.

Won Bok—This tall, pale green celery cabbage is similar in appearance to romaine lettuce. It has a delicate, mild flavor and is also known as Chinese cabbage.

Won Ton—A dumpling made with won ton pi which is filled and deep-fried, steamed, or cooked soft in soup.

Index

Contributors

The Committee for *A Taste of Aloha*

Cherye Pierce and Ann Ellis .... Co-Chairmen 1982-83
Carole Wilbur .... Chairman 1980-82
Lynn Blakely .... Editor
Marianne Dymond and Pam Gough .... Marketing Co-Chairmen
Gretchen Hack, Lynette Char and Nancy Freeman .... Typists

Committee Members
1982 83
Diane Ackerson
Coe Atherton
Bambi D'Olier
Sara Dudgeon
Susan Friedl
Sally Habermeyer
Bayanne Hauhart
Liz Howard
Nancy Goessling
Laurie Lawson
Dianne Lee
Carol McNamee
Sally Mist
Chris O'Brien
Kathy Richardson
Debbie Robertson
Sally Schmid
Betty Stickney
Marianne Vaughan

Special thanks to:
Albert Schmid
Lois Taylor
Bertie Lee

Lila Pang
Margo Stahl
Cleo Evans
Mitch D'Olier
Jean Durkee
Jay Frost
Dee Helber

Contributors
Joan Aanavi
Bob Ackerson
Diane Ackerson
Elizabeth Adams
Corine Albright
Bonnie Andrew
Mary Atchison
Coe Atherton
Lauren Avery
Debra Bauer*
Casey Beck
Mary Ann Bell
Koby Berrington
Constance Black
Cecelia Blackfield
Lynn Blakely
Audrey Bliss

Decie Blitz
Nancy Boyle
Elizabeth Boynton
Joan Bring
Beth Broadbent
Janice Broderick
Jane Bums
Margaret Cameron
Merilyn Cannon
Jean Carlsmith
Jane Carney
Carol Case
Gerry Ching
Philip Ching
Becky Connable
Vivienne Cooke
Mary Cooke
Briar Cornuelle*
Phyllis Corteway
Bee Cromwell*
Dicki Davis
Anita DeDomenico
Diane Dericks
Beth Devereux
Mary Ann Dickie
Bambi D'Olier

Linda Dreher
Sara Dudgeon
Marcia Duff
Margie Durant
Barbara Dwyer
Ann Ellis
Mary Ellis
Marti Erickson
Charlotte Farrell
Patricia Faus
Lesley Ferguson
Connie Flattery
Susan Forman
Pam Freed
Nancy Freeman
Susan Friedl
Lisa Gibson
Trish Glen
Nancy Goessling
Nancy Goodale
Marilyn Goss
Rae Gresso
Lynda Gruver
Sally Habermeyer
Tooty Hager
Leonia Halsey
Renee Hampton
Puddi Hastings
Bayanne Hauhart
Patricia Hemmeter
Sue Hendry
Anne Hoadley*
Jeanne Hoffman
Allison Holland
Donna Hoshide
Liz Howard
Mina Humphreys
Helen Hurtig
Patty Inaba
Dana Izumi
Susan Jacobs*
Claire Johnson
Lila Johnson
Margot Johnson

Claire Jones
Jackie Jones
Bonnie Judd
Delores Judd
Sally Judd
Geneal Kanalz
Jean Kellerman
Marie Kelley*
Kristi Kendig
Adrienne King
Hilda Kitagawa
Grace Kobayashi
Mary Kondo
Janet Larsen
Mary Pat Larsen
Tina Lau
Laurie Lawson
Betsy LaTorre
Buzzy Lee
Dianne Lee
Bertie Lee
Mary Lou Lewis
Dee Lum
Cindy Lupton
Teri Machado
Ginny Maciszewski*
Barbara Marumoto
Susan Matthews
Leslie Mattice
Wendy Maxwell
Linda McCabe
Nancy McKibbin
Carol McNamee
Kay McWayne
Peggy Melim
D.C. Mist
Sally Mist
Meredith Moncata
Kaye Moore
Sis Moore
Sharon Morton
Martha Lee Mullen
Margo Mun
Mary Murdy

Teruo Nakama
Pat Neufeldt
Betty Nicholson
Lucille Nimitz
Chris O'Brien
Fran Osborne
Sybil Padgett
Lila Pang
Maggie Parkes
Cherye Pierce
Jim Pierce
Becky Pietsch
Judy Pietsch
Mele Pochevera
Gail Potter
Bonnie Prior
Helja Pruyn
Elizabeth Pump
Mary Richards
Kathy Richardson
Tetta Richert
Jiggs Ritchie
Debbie Robertson
Lei Saito
Mabel Saito
Sally Schmid
Pat Schnack
Bobby Lou Schneider
Sadye Shayer
Dianne Simmons
Donna Singlehurst
Jorgen Skov
Jean Smith
Rebecca Snider-Norris
Diana Snyder
Margo Sorenson
Walton Stansell*
Polly Steiner
Melissa Stevens
Betty Stickney
Paulette Stone*
Mary Anne
  Stubenberg
Trudie Taylor

Pat Tharp
Susan Thom
Rande Thompkins
Vonnie Turner
Lynn Turner
Marianne Vaughan
Pattie Wagner
Sybil Watson

Lynn Werner
Carolyn Whitney
Carole Wilbur
Norma Wilbur
Mary Wilson
Carolyn Wolfberg
Barbara Wong
Cyndi Wong

Lou Woolley
Kathy Wright
Andy Yim
Eva Zane

**Past Committee
Members*

The Committee for *Another Taste of Aloha*

Davina Chun-Hom and Julie Ra-Goodman ....Co-Chairpersons 1991-92
Gail Makinodan and Linda Naviaux ....Co-Chairpersons 1992-93
Robbie Dingeman and Suzanne Peterson ....Co-Chairpersons 1993-94
Tracy C. Jones ....Editor
Kell Douglas ....Recipe Coordinator
Anne Anderson ....Art Director

Experts
Dominique Jamain
  (Kahala Hilton)
Thomas Ky (Assaggio
  Italian Restaurant)
George
  Mavrothalassitis
  (Halekulani)
Gary Strehl (Hawaii
  Prince Hotel)
Pacific Broiler
Lois Taylor
Bess Press, Inc.

Committee Members
1991-1993
Mary Mau
Erin Oshita Choy
Karen Ono
Mary Keller
Lissa Dunford
Kelly Cross
Chris Lau
Aileen Saito
Sherry Wilfong

Liz Grindle
Jean Hamakawa
Linda Martell
Alana Cline
Elizabeth Stillion
Beth Worrall-Daily
Jodi Maero
Deborah Lau
  Okamura
Gloria Morgan
Laurie Okamoto
Kathy Rueter
Debbie Wong
Rhonda Vadset
Paulette Yoshida
Marcia Warren

Advisor
Sally Mist
(and honorary
committee members:
Wakey, McKibbin
and Billy Mist)

Contributors
Valerie Adams
Debbie Ahern
Shirlee Albrecht
Lucy Alexander
Amelia Andrade
Julie Ang
Cary Anzai
Amy Arapoff
Lynn Arimoto
Ann Armistead
Anne Asper-Davis
Alisa Au
Debby Atkinson
Cherie Axelrod
Martha Balkin
Helena Barahal
Carmen Basa
Mary Baumgardner
K.J. Bell
Margo Berg
Mary Begier
Mary Bershard
Valerie Blaisdell
Nancy Biller

Marita Collins Biven
Tess Blanco
Ann Botticelli
Bernice Bowers
Nancy Boyle
Kathy Brondes
Maureen Buckley
Sherri Bulkley
Lynne Bunch
Mary Burke
Beth Reaves
    Burroughs
Kathy Cabreros
Kimberly Caldwell
Phoebe Campbell
Merilyn Cannon
Christina Carlson
Connie Carr
Jane Carney
Sarah Casken
Fredrica Cassiday
Barbara Champion
Ellie Champion
Susie Childs
Sharon Ching
Cynthia Christensen
Kathy Christensen
Carl Choy
Liz Chun
Clayton Chun-Hom
Kathy Clifford
Terry Clifton
Janice Cole
Joanie Colman
Nancy Conley
Lore Cook
Jacqueline Corteway
Phyllis Corteway
Kathy Crandall
Heidi Cregor
Doris Crow
Patricia Culver
Diane Damon
Joan Danieley

Dottie Darrow
Dori Davis
Katie Desmarais
Gary Dias
Josephine B.
    Dingeman
Maria Di Tullio
Lindsay Dodge
Mary Jo Eline
Ann Fairfax Ellett
Jane Emerson-Brown
Krystal Emge
Wendy Farley
Pam Felix
Shelley Fernandez
Holly Fiocca
Susan Flowers
Julia Fong
Cynthia Fragale
C.R. Glenn
Laura Glenn
Jan Gordon
Beverley S. Grimmer
Judy Grimes
Randy Grobe
Anna Grune
Nancy Gurczyneski
Rhoda Hackler
Claire Hagenbuch
Lisa Hayashi
Carolyn Heitzman
Robin Park Helms
Lisa Hemmeter
Kim Hemmeter
Tina Henry
Mavis Higa
Sono Hirose-Hulbert
Nona Holmes
Missy Holmes
Kathy Hong
Tina Louise Hoogs
Catherine Howieson
Mina Humphreys
Debra Hunt

Mollie Hustace
Rona Ikehara
Dana Izumi
Krissy Izumi
Tracy Jaconette
Jackie Johnson
Lila Johnson
Claire Johnson
Stephanie Johnson
Jeffrie Jones
Susan Kamida
Mary Ann Kelly
Paula Kelly
Doug Kilpatrick
Karen Kimbrell
Adrienne King
Julie King
Ann Klaug
Dale Klein
Dawn Krause
Laura Konda
Diane Kudo
Elizabeth Lacy
Lyn Lam
Amy Lamparello
Elizabeth B. Lee
Lennie Lee
Sherree Lee
Susan Leong
Melissa Lewis
Amy Li
Robin Liu
Georgia Locks
John Locks
Ben Locquiao
Shannon Lowrey
Joseph Lovell
Ann Lozada
Rita Luppino
Kimberly Luyckx
Victoria Lyman
Andrea Lyon
Helen MacNeil
Dorothy Manly

Barbara Marumoto
Kim Marumoto
Susu Markham
Mary Marx
Betty Mastrantonio
Lenora Matsuda
Nancy Maxwell
Wendy Maxwell
Amy McCormack
Lieala McCullen
Teresa McDonald
Madeleine McKay
Vera McKenzie
Kay McWayne
Nancy Meguro
Laura Mellow
P. Merillat
Pat Metcalf
Naomi Mihara
Gerry Milnor
Lisa Moore
Susan Moore
Susan Morrill
Julie Ann Morris
Shannon Morrison
DeEtte Mountford
Margo Mun
Lisa Munger
Myrna Murdoch
Jessica Myrabo
Cindy Nichols
Maggie O Brien
Suzanne and Warren
   O'Donell
Carolyn O 'Keefe
Hae Okimoto
Cary Olin
Nancy O'Malley
Maile Ostrem
Carol Lee Owens
Sandy Pablo
Nancy Pace
Sybil Padgett
Lou Parsons

Shelley Pasko
Barbara Petrus
Barbara Phillips
Beryl Pierce
Kathy Prenger
Darnney Proudfoot
Melissa Goldsmith
   Pryor
Eileen Quinn
Lori Rand
Susan Rehberg-
   Merrill
Donna Reid-Hayes
Allene Richardson
Pokey Richardson
Debbie Robertson
Lori Roberts-Mitchell
Ellen Roos-Marr
Cathy Rungee
Kathy Sabota
Aileen Saito
Mary Saunders
Lissa Schiff
Lori Schlueter
Cynthia Schnack
Mari-Jo Schull
Laurel Schuster
Menakoki Schwan
Julie B. Schwarz
Val Schweigert
Tina Semenza
Monica Shaney
Sharon Shanley
Pat Shimizu
Lisa Siegfried
Sara Silverman
Cheryl Sisler
Julie Sloane
Celeste Smith
Diana Snyder
Katy Soldner
Irish Sonnenberg
Susan Soong
Karen Sotomura

Aileen Stephanos
Nancy Stephenson
Peggy Stitham
Karen Sumner
Anne Swank
Betty Swindle
Diana Snyder
Corinne Takasaki
Cynthia Thielen
Nicki Thompson
Penelope Thune
Lynne Tokumaru
Gay Tsukamaki
Mindy Tucker
Karen Turran
June Udell
Carol Vieira
Marcia Warren
Jojo Watumull
Mary Wessberg
Lael Wheeler
Theresa Whitaker
Tookie White
Kari Wilhite
Elizabeth Wiser
Susan Witten
Cynthia Wo
Paulette Wo
Cyndi Wright Wong
Sandy Wong
Vicki Woolford
Karen Wright
Linda Wright Wong
Leslie Wynhoff
Ruthann Yamanaka
Debbie Yee
Andrea Yip
Annie Yonashiro
Paulette Yoshida
Patti Young
Debra Yuen

The Committees for *Aloha Days Hula Nights*

2003-2004

Carole Berg ....Chair

Vanessa Applbaum	Tracy Jones	Wendy Shewalter
Lurlyn Brown	Coral Rasmussen	

2004-2005

Carole Berg ....Chair

Heather Ardoin	Suzanne Lee	Barbara Sniezek
Monique Canonico	Kristi Nicholson	Susan Worley
Tracy Jones	Coral Rasmussen	
Melinda Kohr	Wendy Shewalter	

2005-2006

Tanya Hertel, Austen Cook, Carole Berg....................................Co-Chairs

Dianne Bosworth	Tracy Jones	Oleana Sagapolutele
Lurlyn Brown	Melinda Kohr	Wendy Shewalter
Jodie Ching	Nancy Page	Susan Worley
Marisa Gumpfer	Coral Rasmussen	
Heather Henken	Nina Pfaffenbach	

2006-2007

Carrie Allport, Lee Ann Del Carpio, Anna Grisi..........................Co-Chairs

Carole Berg ....Advisor

Dianne Bosworth	Heather McDermott	John DeMello
Sue Chouljian	Nancy Page	Robert C. Godbey
Marisa Gumpfer	Rose Smith	Lorry Kennedy
Tracy Jones	Kimi Takazawa	Dick Lyday
Melinda Kohr		
Lauren Lewis	**Special thanks to:**	Nina Pfaffenbach
Lisa Matsuda	Buzz Belknap	

About the Artist

Pegge Hopper was born in Oakland, CA. She studied painting at the Los Angeles Art Center College of Design. In 1956, she worked in New York for Raymond Loewy Associates.

Living in Milan, Italy from 1961-1963, she was an illustrator for laRinascente.

Pegge came to Honolulu in 1963 and was an art director for a local agency. After visiting the State Archives and seeing old photographs of native Hawaiians, she was inspired to start painting again.

Her gallery opened in 1983 in Honolulu's Historic Chinatown.